50 Ways to Love Your Life
Sarah Cline, Ph.D.

Copyright © 2024 by Sarah Cline, Ph.D.

All rights reserved.

Contents

Introduction   1

1. The Power of Positivity   3
   The Benefits of Positive Thinking
   Ways to Cultivate Positivity
   Key Takeaways

2. Communicate with Yourself and Others   8
   Learn What It Means to Communicate
   Learn How to Listen
   Communicate to Understand—Not to Respond
   Express Your Emotions with Yourself and Others
   Learn What It Means to Be Compassionate
   Forgive and Make Peace with the Past
   Communicate Boundaries—and Steer Clear of Those Who Cross Them
   Find Out What Makes You Tick
   Have Emotional Check-Ins with Yourself and Others
   Know and Communicate Your Limits
   Key Takeaways

3. Appreciate Your Family and Friends—and Yourself   36
    Nurture Positive Relationships
    Avoid Toxic Relationships
    Keep Commitments
    Treat Loved Ones to R&R
    Plan an Adventure
    Experience New Hobbies
    Travel Somewhere New
    Cherish Memories
    Connect Deeply with Others
    Show You Care with Surprises
    Key Takeaways

4. Keep Yourself Healthy   60
    Do Activities You Enjoy
    Go to the Doctor Regularly
    Eat Nutritious Foods and Hydrate
    Maintain Proper Hygiene
    Meditate/Pray
    Take Care of Your Dental and Eye Care
    Limit Screen Time
    Take More Naps
    Fill Your Time with Things That Matter
    Properly Manage Your Emotions
    Key Takeaways

5. Live in the Moment   81

    Buy Yourself Things That Make You Happy

    Make Time to Laugh!

    Splurge on Things Occasionally

    Express Yourself Artistically

    Create a Bucket List

    Key Takeaways

6. Socialize and Experience Joy   95

    Identify Your Role Models

    Quiet the Inner Critic

    Go out and Meet New People

    Go On Dates—With Yourself and Others

    Do Something for Someone in Need

    Key Takeaways

7. Celebrate   109

    Approach Every Day Like It Could Be the Best Day of Your Life

    Start a Gratitude Journal

    Appreciate the Journey

    Celebrate Special Days

    Make Traditions Together

    Get Together with Loved Ones

    Learn New Ways to Unwind and Enjoy Life

    Find Ways to Make Every Day Special

    Consciously Work to Be Positive

    Always Work to Learn and Develop Yourself

Key Takeaways

8. Final Thoughts   127

About the Author   130

Introduction

Welcome to "50 Ways to Love Your Life," a little guide designed to help you discover the joy, fulfillment, and satisfaction that your life has to offer. In these pages, you'll find insights, techniques, and inspiration to cultivate a deeper appreciation for the beauty and richness of life, including how to not only appreciate what you have already but also to build upon it.

Life is a journey filled with ups and downs, twists and turns, but within every moment lies the potential for growth, connection, and joy. Whether you're seeking to enhance or strengthen your relationships, improve your overall state of being, or simply find more meaning and purpose in your normal everyday existence, this book is here to act as a compass.

You will learn that through the exploration of positivity, communication, relationships, health, mindfulness, joy, and celebration, you can uncover the keys to unlocking a life filled with a *lot* to be grateful for—leading to an abundance of contentment and enjoyment for years to come. Each chapter should offer valuable insight and practical strategies to help you navigate challenges with grace and resilience to live life to its fullest.

As you embark on this journey, remember that the path to loving your life is unique to you. Embrace each lesson with an open mind and a willing heart, and trust that by investing in yourself and prioritizing what truly matters, you'll create a life that brings you deep fulfillment and happiness.

So, without further ado, let's dive in and discover fifty ways to love your life—together.

Chapter 1

The Power of Positivity

Imagine waking up each morning with a sense of excitement and anticipation for the day that lies ahead of you. Picture feeling energized, motivated, and ready to tackle whatever challenges come your way, rather than sluggish and groggy. This is the power of positivity—the ability to approach life with optimism can truly turn even the most mundane situations into opportunities for growth and fulfillment.

In this chapter, we explore the profound psychological benefits of maintaining a positive outlook on your everyday life. From improved mental and physical well-being to enhanced relationships and greater resilience in the face of adversity, merely being positive about life and its circumstances has the potential to enrich every aspect of your life. The hope is that once you read through this chapter, you will have the knowledge and expertise to cultivate a more powerful mindset so that you can breathe more positivity and embrace each day from now on with enthusiasm and gratitude.

The Benefits of Positive Thinking

Of course, we all know it's better to be positive. We have heard it throughout our lifetimes. But why is it important to try and remain positive?

Research has shown that taking on a positive outlook can have a huge impact on our mental and physical health. Focusing on the good things in your life, rather than the negative, you open the door to:

- **Reduced stress and anxiety:** Lower levels of stress hormones such as cortisol, as well as reduced symptoms of anxiety and depression, have been linked to those with a more positive outlook. This suggests that cultivating a more optimistic mindset in our daily lives offers a better coping mechanism to life's challenges, which can, in turn, aid in navigating stressful situations with greater ease.

- **Improved physical health:** Overall better health comes from positivity too! Studies have shown a link between being positive and having lower blood pressure, stronger immune function, and even a reduction in heart disease and stroke risk.

- **Greater resilience:** Just because you're positive doesn't mean you ignore the fact that problems do exist or that you go through life with rose-colored glasses. It merely involves approaching life's challenges with a mindset full of resilience and optimism. When you maintain a positive outlook, you can quickly bounce back from setbacks, which then allows you to overcome obstacles.

- **Stronger relationships:** Being a Debbie Downer usually is a turnoff for others. Having and maintaining a positive attitude can improve our relationships because it makes us more approachable, and besides, happy people enjoy the company of other happy people. Attitude is often contagious.

Ways to Cultivate Positivity

While some individuals may naturally possess a sunny disposition, being positive is actually a skill that can be cultivated and developed over time. And fortunately for all of those naturally pessimistic folks out there, there are techniques and exercises to help you foster a more positive outlook on life:

- **Practice gratitude:** First and foremost, it is important to take each day as it is and spend a few moments each day reflecting on things you are grateful for. It's easy to focus on the negative, but switch gears and take a look around. Is it a beautiful day? Is it your friends, family, or significant other? Maybe you're getting that takeout dish you have been craving all week. Whatever the case, make sure you note the good. Keeping a gratitude journal can be a powerful way to do this.

- **Reframe negative thoughts:** Setbacks happen. When you're faced with them, try reframing the thoughts in a way that's more positive. Rather than dwelling on what went wrong, try and focus on something you learned instead—and how you might grow and improve in the future.

- **Surround yourself with positivity:** Try and find something that makes you feel good about your situation. Music, books, or spending time with loved ones are all great sources of inspiration. By surrounding yourself with these positive forces, you help reinforce optimism.

- **Practice self-care:** This is something often forgotten because we, as a society, have placed a "selfishness" stigma on regular self-care. However, taking care of your physical, emotional, and mental well-being is crucial for maintaining a positive outlook. You have to make time for activities that bring you joy and relaxation, otherwise you'll feel burned out and oftentimes garner depression. So, no matter what it is that you find helps—whether it's going for a walk in nature, prayer, meditation, or indulging in hobbies—make sure that you make time for those types of enjoyment.

Key Takeaways

"Chapter 1: The Power of Positivity" underscores the potential of positivity in daily life and how it might be quite easily one of the biggest cornerstones of learning to love your life. By embracing optimism, individuals can enhance their mental and physical well-being, foster stronger relationships, and build resilience, even in the face of adversity.

Maintaining a positive outlook has been linked to reduced stress and anxiety levels, improved physical health, greater resilience, and stronger interpersonal connections. This means that positivity has some huge power, and although some people may naturally possess a positive disposition, positivity is a skill that can be developed over time. Techniques such as practicing gratitude, reframing negative thoughts, surrounding yourself with positive influences, and prioritizing self-care can all aid in fostering a more optimistic mindset. By integrating these practices into daily life, you can harness the power of positivity and navigate challenges with resilience, appreciate life's blessings, and approach each day with a newfound love.

Chapter 2

Communicate with Yourself and Others

Effective communication is the foundation of any healthy relationship and, therefore, a cornerstone in maintaining a happy and healthy life. Human beings are social creatures, and no matter how introverted you may be, you still need others in your life to be happy and productive. Regardless of if it is a romantic relationship or a relationship with your best friend, communication is necessary. It is the bridge that connects us all and enables us to come to a mutual understanding and build a stronger bond with one another.

In this chapter, we'll delve into the essential components of communication that can strengthen the bond you have with your friend. Moreover, the chapter will navigate the traits of each personality type and how you can use personality indicators to validate your friend, yourself, and both of your needs.

While it's easy to be swayed by the idea that love is a mysterious force beyond our control, the reality is that maintaining a lasting relationship requires a lot more than just love. It requires conscious effort, respect, and a willingness to understand one another on a deeper level. This journey of appreciation goes beyond knowing your friend's favorite "things" or doing what you think will make them "happy." It's about diving deep into their psyche (and yours), comprehending their unique personality traits (and yours), and recognizing how their attributes interact with yours in a way that can formulate a healthy and lasting relationship.

In the age of digital connections and instant gratification, we sometimes forget the beauty of human interaction. We often overlook the importance of patience, reflection, and presence with our loved ones. At times, we also let external factors beyond that pull us away from what truly matters. Thus, you can pause, reflect, and feel as we progress through this chapter. By fostering an environment of open communication and mutual respect, you're not just building relationships and bonds but cultivating relationships that thrive on understanding, compassion, and genuine connection. Using this guide, you can learn how to not just communicate with your friend, but these are some strategies and ground rules to help you convey your emotions effectively.

Learn What It Means to Communicate

To find a true connection in any relationship, you must first be able to communicate. Human connection is critical, and the quality of that connection—no matter the relationship—depends on how much meaning we derive from the communication we have with them.

Relationship building is facilitated by meaningful communication. None of us want to feel isolated or disconnected or be knee-deep in relationships with those who don't value us emotionally. By working to develop both strength in relationships and building supportive environments all around, we can offset a degree of pain or unhappiness in ourselves—and others' lives.

The good news is that communication is a skill set. We can learn and apply strategies to build better relationships, as well as gain greater depth of meaning and emotional connection inside these relationships.

Learn How to Listen

Communicating is fundamentally a shared process between two or more people. It's a two-way street. You are never going to be the only one talking, which also means it will eventually be your turn to listen as well. Think about how much you want to feel heard when you speak to others. The other person likely wants to feel heard just as much. Although it may feel counterintuitive, don't start with talking in your conversations. Start with listening. This is because listening is validating to the other person. And if you *are* a talker—don't worry! Your turn will come.

It's also important to acknowledge that being skilled at listening means being aware that there may be more under the surface—more than what's being said. Instead of making assumptions about what you see or hear, understand that it is important that you have clarity. The full scope of proper listening should include:

- **Giving your undivided attention:** Put the phone down and minimize other distractions or interruptions. If you are stressed or anxious, then regulate your breathing to relax. You can't focus on them if your mind is swirling with anxieties. Be prepared to reorient your attention back to the person you're listening to if your thoughts waver.

- **Being supportive:** When someone is speaking, and it's clear that they need support—offer it to them! Use your words and your body language to show that you are engaged. This encourages them to continue and shows them that you're truly listening to what they have to say.

- **Being empathic:** Empathy means to understand someone else's situation from their point of view. It's okay to disagree with someone, but learn to let go of preconceived ideas and wait while they explain their perspective so you can understand where they're coming from. You can better state your position once you understand theirs.

- **Being patient:** Let them set the pace of the conversation. Don't interrupt them, or finish their sentences, and never speak in a way that makes them feel like they need to rush.

- **Going beyond words:** Sometimes, nonverbal cues, such as the body language of the other person, provide information. Look for facial expressions, body gestures, and eye movements for more detail about what they're saying.

- **Finding the big picture:** Remember that the person speaking is communicating their ideas with you. Take all the information provided to you (verbally and nonverbally) and ask follow-up questions as necessary. Make sure that you understand the big picture.

Communicate to Understand—Not to Respond

One of the biggest hurdles that people face when it comes to arguments is their communication styles. More specifically, if one or both parties lack proper listening skills. Often, you may hear someone's words but still have no clue what they really mean. Being a good listener means going beyond that, as we just discussed. Think about it—if you are not really listening, then most of the conversations you're having are one-sided, meaning there is more opportunity to lose what someone else's intentions are. This creates conflict based around miscommunication because you're really having your own conversation if you stop listening to the other person or begin implanting your own ideas into the conversation where they wouldn't be present if you just harbored better listening skills.

So, how do you know if you need to improve your listening skills? Some of the biggest indicators are the following:

- You get frustrated that someone is taking "too long" to speak.

- Your loved one says, "You don't get it" often.

- Your loved one says, "You aren't listening," or "That's not what I said."

All of these can indicate deeper problems with listening. Another thing to look out for is your own self-interest. It's human nature. When something is interesting, we are more apt to listen versus when we are bored. When you're bored, your listening skills quickly deteriorate, and that is completely normal. However, if you want to improve your relationships, you must try to shift gears when it comes to your listening skills.

- **Suspend our own agenda:** Stop focusing on what you're going to say while they're talking. You can't listen if you're worried about how to respond.

- **Be interested:** This may be easier said than done. However, if you care for the person speaking, you should have somewhat of an interest in how they're feeling about a particular situation. Focus on their feelings.

- **Be a reporter:** Sometimes, when you're communicating and you are trying to boost your listening skills, it helps to pretend you're a reporter, and you have to know enough to write about it. Take mental notes (or physical ones if it's appropriate to do so).

- **Ask questions:** This also helps engage your loved one when they're speaking. When you follow up with questions, you're not only gaining clarity for something you may not understand, but you're also showing that you are listening and invested in the conversation and understanding where they're coming from.

- **Make eye contact and use minimal encouragers:** This also helps with not being distracted. If you're looking at their eyes, you're not looking at your phone or other people or things that may distract you from the conversation. Just as you're reading their body language, they're reading yours. Use minimal encouragers verbally to show them that not only are you undistracted and looking at them, but you're also encouraging them to continue with what it is that they are saying.

- **Avoid judgment:** Whether you agree or not does not matter. Focus more on understanding their perspective and find out why they feel the way they do without imparting judgment—besides, you don't know what their message is completely if you interrupt mid-sentence. Interrupting is a waste of time. It not only can frustrate your loved one but also make you lose the trajectory of the information.

- **Don't give unsolicited advice:** One of the biggest takeaways you can have when looking to improve your listening skills is that when someone is speaking to you about something important, they always want you to fix it or give your advice. Sometimes, people just want to vent or communicate their stance. If they ask for your advice, give it—if not, don't give advice. Just be there.

- **Avoid defensiveness:** Focus on their perspective for the time being. Not yours. Once they finish, you can take the appropriate time needed to respond, especially if you have somehow felt attacked by what they've said.

- **Take responsibility:** Act on what has been said. If your loved one has communicated with you something about yourself—even if it's been difficult to hear—take some responsibility for it. You may need to defend yourself, but take the proper time to reflect to know if the defense is warranted or not. Sometimes, an apology is necessary instead. Sometimes, though, you will need to defend yourself or explain yourself if you feel you're being judged too harshly. Just make sure the proper care is taken. However, if, after the conversation, you realize that you do need to make changes—make sure you do so. Meaningful conversation will lose its power if loved ones cannot trust you to apply what has been shared.

- **Follow up with questions:** Our personal feelings, our own assumptions, judgments, or beliefs can often distort what we hear someone saying. As the listener, your role is to understand what is truly being said. This may require you to reflect and ask appropriate questions or retell what they just told you to ensure you understood. Summarize what you heard.

Express Your Emotions with Yourself and Others

Everyone has emotions. It's natural. Expressing them, however, isn't something that's always easy. Getting in touch with your feelings can not only help you understand, but it can also help others understand you better, too.

In fact, being understood and accepted are universal needs that we have—we, as humans, crave that kind of connection. So, when you share your experiences and emotions with others, you're more likely to connect in deep and meaningful ways with them. You're also more likely to get your needs met, which in turn leads to happier and healthier relationships overall.

Don't misunderstand—sharing your feelings *can* be a daunting proposition. When you share your feelings, you allow yourself to be vulnerable. This vulnerability can be scary; after all, it leaves you open to the possibility of being hurt, but it can also lead to the deepest connections.

Understand Your Own Feelings

Before you can express your feelings, you, yourself, have to know what they are. For most people, it helps to have some quiet time to reflect, especially if you aren't naturally intuitive to feelings or emotions. Try taking ten minutes per day for the sole purpose of contemplating how you feel about your life, certain situations, etc. at the present time. Try to identify your feelings, remembering that you can have more than one feeling at once. Explore what's been happening in your life that may be related to your feelings.

Be Selective with Who You Share With

Your feelings are intimate parts of yourself; they shouldn't be shared with just *anyone*. The truth of the matter is that there are times when it's appropriate to be vulnerable with others and times when it isn't. Additionally, there are also times when certain people are not meant to forge a deep connection with others. Make sure that you proceed slowly and begin by sharing feelings that feel safer and less vulnerable before diving in head-first, especially if you aren't the type to generally share intimate details with yourself. If those small vulnerabilities are received well, share a little bit more and go from there.

Respond—Don't React!

Sometimes, we make the mistake of trying to communicate our feelings in a moment of heightened emotion when we aren't regulated. This tends to result in blurting things out before we have processed them or even so much as had the chance to calm down—which leads to miscommunication, stating untruth, or pointing fingers. Basically, it's just not the best time to communicate your emotions. Take the time, regulate, and come back to the conversation.

It is perfectly acceptable to ask to take a break from a heated conversation or wait until you have had time to calm down and prepare what you need to discuss.

Make Sure the Time Is Right

Be intentional about when you try to communicate your feelings, too! Think about who you are trying to communicate with and their schedule. Oftentimes, people try to communicate their needs at the wrong times. You never want it to be while the other person is distracted, busy, under the influence, sleepy, or even just in a poor mood. Sometimes, this means planning ahead and asking for time to be set aside.

In general, make sure that you also try to communicate face-to-face. Technology is convenient, but remember that sometimes context is lost in the written word—and besides, it's less personal and vulnerable. The entire point is deepening the connection.

Be Direct

Understand that effective communication is clear and direct. It's easier to be direct when you know what you're going to say. Plan your conversation—or at least talking points.

Pay Attention to Body Language and Tone

We have discussed a bit of body language in the previous sections. When communicating, body language is just as important as what you're verbally communicating, and so is the tone in which you are speaking. Sometimes, it's difficult to gauge the tone of your own voice. Sometimes, we raise our voices without realizing it or close ourselves off with our facial expressions and body language—even if we want to communicate appropriately. Be aware of how you're coming across to others when communicating.

Learn What It Means to Be Compassionate

Sharing feelings is a part of all relationships, no matter if they're friendships, romantic, or familial. In all healthy relationships, you care about each other's feelings and strive to meet each other's needs. It all needs to be reciprocal. In order to do all of this, it's important to tap into your compassion.

Compassion and empathy are different—yet closely related. Empathy is our feeling of awareness and our attempt at putting ourselves in their shoes. Compassion is an emotional response to that empathy and having a desire to help. Empathy is simply understanding the shared humanity that we have with another person, whereas compassion adds another dimension.

Forgive and Make Peace with the Past

Do you ever find yourself stuck in a cycle of dwelling on past events or traumas, replaying conversations long over with, or even regretting decisions you previously made? It's a common struggle, feeling like you're trapped in a time loop where the past holds more power over you than the present does. Breaking free from this pattern is not only possible but also necessary for personal growth and happiness. Let's explore some practical steps to liberate you from the grip of the past and embrace the potential of the here and now.

Imagine walking down a busy sidewalk right smack dab in the middle of a city, surrounded by the hustle and bustle of life. Each street you pass holds memories, both good and bad, but you slow down to dwell on them so long that you're knocked backward by the crowd. You can no longer move forward. You're stuck. Staring at the past.

Instead of being tethered to yesterday, let go of it. Remember it. Cherish the experiences and lessons. But let go of it—especially the bad. Of course, it's important to gain perspective from the past and continue forward in a healthy way.

Forgive others for their wrongdoings. This does not mean that you have to entertain having them in your life. In fact, if there is trauma there, and steps haven't been made to form a healthy, flourishing relationship—you shouldn't have them in your life.

Breaking free from the past and forgiveness is not about ignoring or denying what has happened; it's about accepting it and moving forward with purpose and resilience. You will feel free to have a wonderful opportunity to love your life.

Communicate Boundaries—and Steer Clear of Those Who Cross Them

Knowing how to set boundaries is one of the most essential yet overlooked social skills there is. For some reason, as human beings, we feel guilty for setting boundaries. We make it seem more rooted in selfishness rather than love, but in all reality, boundaries are necessary in all relationships and must be communicated.

Set Appropriate Boundaries and Change Them as Relationships Evolve

Boundaries are "fences" or "lines" that are critical. Setting boundaries is an act that paves the way for understanding and respect. Our friends and family often help us figure out who we are, and they're there for us when things are difficult. They also share our joys and successes. However, there are also times when your relationship dynamics change or when each of you evolves, whether together or independently of one another. Boundaries need to be re-established as things change.

Learn to Say No

If you're a "yes" person, that's great. However, learning how to say "no" is a critical first step in setting boundaries. Saying "yes" continually in any relationship is a great way to feel overwhelmed eventually, which can lead to burnout. This can be detrimental to your relationships as you can start to resent your loved ones in the future. Don't do things that make you uncomfortable or that you just don't feel you want to do. You don't have to say "no" all the time, especially if you're a people pleaser, but consider mixing it in from time to time, especially when necessary to your mental or physical health. Remember, a true loved one will leave space for you to give yourself a little self-care. A "no" will never compromise a healthy relationship.

Redirect

Difficult conversations have to happen sometimes. Boundary setting can be a particularly challenging conversation at that, so much so that you don't want to do it more than once if you can help it. Communicating your boundaries effectively the first time can curb the need to redirect, but sometimes, it may be necessary. For instance, if you have set a boundary in which you would prefer your loved one not to complain about someone else the two of you know, and they do anyway, try to redirect the conversation. Instead of yelling at them for crossing your boundary, attempt to redirect them. Simply saying something like, "I'm sorry everything is difficult between the two of you, but let's talk about something else." This can typically give them enough insight to understand that you're not interested in continuing the conversation. If they press further, stand your ground and be even more stern.

Don't Be Afraid to Ask for What You Need

No matter how you spin it, people are not mind readers. No matter how much your friend or family member knows you, they won't know exactly what you need unless you ask for it. A really useful skill in life is finding ways to state a need in a respectful way. In fact, this is a tool that will benefit you across all relationships, which includes friendships, romantic relationships, and even your professional ones. Letting people know what you need (such as solidarity or space) allows people the chance to respect that request. Without your communication, they might not have the ability to realize that was something you needed and could have overwhelmed you without meaning to. By communicating your need for solidarity/space, you have successfully avoided conflict or hard feelings.

Validate and Reaffirm

When you first have a "boundary" discussion with someone, it can be truly difficult. It's easy to worry that someone will be hurt, but it's important to understand that there are ways to improve everyone's experience during this conversation. By practicing open dialogue with your loved one, you will be able to develop a sense of how to express yourself to them positively. Reaffirm your love for them, what it is that they do right, and what you enjoy about them. Affirmations can really reinforce that trust, and that, in turn, makes the conversation a lot more palatable.

Be Direct

Some people may have difficulty with this at first, but it truly is the best policy. Skirting around the subject can often lead to misunderstandings and confusion. Clarity really helps others understand where you are and what you need. They need to understand where they stand with you. At the end of the day, there can be pain and hurt feelings just by wondering this. Besides, your loved one is likely to be more perceptive in hearing something from you in a direct manner, rather than upsetting you later and not knowing why. So, be direct when asking for what you need. You can be kind and respectful and still be clear as glass!

Respect Differences

When you set boundaries for your loved ones, it's important to note that there will be differences in opinion—and they may have a different boundary for you, even on the same subject matter. You may have one boundary for yourself for your loved one to abide by, and they may request something completely different from you. While it's normal to wish that others were different than they are, it is not okay to disrespect their perspective. Issues arise when people become self-righteous, angry, or condescending, especially when dealing with personal boundaries. That is when a situation becomes toxic and potentially abusive.

Diversity can be an absolutely wonderful thing as it makes the world a much more interesting place. Respect your friend's differences, even if those differences can sometimes butt against yours and become frustrating.

Don't Forget "You Time"

In the same boat as self-care is "you time." Giving yourself proper "you" time is essential in setting boundaries. It's all a balance, and although it's admirable to give your whole self to your friends and family, it's often necessary to take a step back to recharge those batteries and do something only for you. "You time" serves as the sanctuary for self-reflection, personal growth, and rejuvenation. It's a deliberate pause—a moment that you can take in order to indulge in activities that bring you joy and fulfillment, as well as recharge your spirit.

Whether it's pursuing hobbies or engaging in solitary activities at home in your pajamas, this time is essential as it carves out space for that self-care and personal introspection.

Prioritizing "you" time not only revitalizes your energy but also contributes to a more enriching and authentic presence within the friendship. How can you be 100 percent for them if you aren't 100 percent for yourself? This intentional investment in your own personal well-being reinforces a healthier approach to the relationship itself, ensuring that while you nurture yourself, you're, in turn, nurturing the connection the two of you have.

Be Consistent

Consistency in your boundaries keeps your expectations clear and focused. It is critical that once you've communicated your boundaries, you remain steadfast in upholding them. Consistency involves honoring your limits regardless of circumstances or external pressures. Don't let someone make you feel guilty for your boundaries. In fact, boundaries are an essential part of a relationship and end up creating a healthy atmosphere for love to prosper. It's crucial to stand by your decisions to maintain respect for your own needs. This fosters a mutually respectful relationship.

It is important that you consistently reinforce your boundaries when necessary. If a friend unknowingly crosses a boundary, gently remind them. Clear and respectful communication reaffirms the importance of these boundaries and helps maintain understanding.

Set Consequences (If Needed)

In situations where boundaries are repeatedly ignored or violated, establish consequences. This doesn't mean immediately ending the relationship, but it might involve reducing interaction or taking a break to reassess the relationship's dynamics. Be communicative if this process ends up needing to happen with your friend.

Prioritize Self-Care

By being consistent in your boundaries, you're also practicing self-care. By focusing on your well-being and not compromising your mental, emotional, or physical health for the sake of avoiding conflict or maintaining a relationship that doesn't respect your limits, you are giving yourself proper care and love. This will only make you better for others, too.

Show Them How to Behave

If boundaries are new with your loved ones, make sure that your behavior aligns with the boundaries you have set for them. You have to show yourself—and them—the same level of respect. For example, if the boundary is about respecting your time, make sure that you respect your own time by not allowing it to be infringed upon. If they're late to leave for a movie, leave without them. Likewise, model that behavior by respecting their time. Don't be late for their plans if you're asking them not to be late for yours.

Seek Support (If Necessary)

If maintaining boundaries becomes challenging or overwhelming, seek support from trusted individuals, such as other friends, a therapist, or a support group. They can provide guidance and encouragement. If you're seeking out support from a nonprofessional, make sure that you're not gossiping about your friend. This can lead to hurt feelings and a lot more conflict than what has already transpired.

Reflect and Adjust When Needed

Periodically reflect on your boundaries and their effectiveness. Assess whether they're serving their purpose in the relationship. Are you happy? Are they? If necessary, make adjustments to your boundaries based on evolving circumstances or changes in your needs. Make sure that you're asking your friend for their input as well. This will help them feel more like a partner in this journey rather than someone abiding by your rules and your rules only.

Celebrate Progress

Acknowledge and celebrate your consistency in upholding boundaries as well as your loved ones respecting them. Recognize the positive impact it has on your well-being and the health of your friendship. Celebrating small victories encourages continued commitment on both of your parts.

Maintain Open Communication

Consistency doesn't mean rigidity. Be open to discussing your boundaries if circumstances change or if there's a need for adjustment. Maintaining open lines of communication allows for a better understanding between the two of you. As stated earlier, ask for feedback and make sure that both of you are communicating evenly so that you can both work, mutually, on your relationship.

Practice Patience

Consistency in boundary setting takes time and effort. It can be incredibly draining because it is a continuous process. However, although it is rigorous and might face challenges, it's worth it in the end if your relationship comes out stronger. Be patient with yourself and with your friend as you both navigate these boundaries together.

Find Out What Makes You Tick

If you've ever been asked the question, "What makes you tick?" you may have found it harder to answer than you realized. But if you don't know—then who will? If you don't know yourself, who knows you? The reason this question is so hard to answer is that we don't often reflect on our own basic thoughts, feelings, or behaviors.

By taking time to reflect on yourself, you can open the door to gathering insight into yourself like never before. It's important to know what you dislike and what makes you uncomfortable so you can express that and not have a loved one in the crossfire.

Have Emotional Check-Ins with Yourself and Others

Emotional check-ins are an important aspect of life. They are not only important so that you can check in with your friends and family and how they feel your relationship is going/or how they are doing in their everyday lives—but emotional check-ins are also good to participate in with yourself.

We live so much of our day outside of ourselves, and it quickly becomes second nature to forget to pull yourself back in and check in with yourself. We engage in conversations with others at work, at home, and even on social media. We read stories, news articles, and the opinions of others almost constantly. And in our downtime, we try to give a little energy to those close to us. It seems our mental space is almost always occupied. But you have to open up a bit of internal conversation—for your own sanity.

Spending time with yourself can sometimes even feel like another task on your miles-long to-do list, but it truly is an essential part of taking care of your emotional wellness and mental health. Just as you would exercise your physical body, "working out" your mind will help keep you balanced even with the stress of day-to-day life.

Checking in with yourself means carving out time every day to ask yourself how you're doing—in life in general, your relationships, your job, etc. In this space, you are afforded an opportunity to sort out your emotions, assess your physical and emotional needs, and make an intentional plan on how to address these needs moving forward.

Self-Reflection Time: Choose a time of day when you're the least likely to be interrupted, turn on your favorite tunes, and have a good think session. People often complete self-reflection time while doing other tasks. Two main ones are:

- **Journaling:** If you express yourself best through the written word (looking at you, list-makers), grab your notebook and set aside a quick daily writing session. Even one minute is better than none.

- **Meditation:** Mindfulness is all about becoming aware of your emotions and watching them pass with nonjudgment. The meditation seat is an excellent place to work on the skill of checking in and letting go.

Emotional Check-Ins with Your Partner

Regular relationship check-ins are a great opportunity with your significant others, too. Especially as you begin to navigate how to truly communicate with one another. They can become a platform to address concerns as well as strengthen your connection with one another, which is a vital tool in your relationship. These check-ins can be as often as you need them to be. Some couples do them every night, some once a week, and some may only check in once a month. Do what works best for your relationship. This may take a little time to find that perfect sweet spot, too, so don't be afraid to ask your partner if they feel you are checking in enough.

No matter how often, it is important to schedule a dedicated time for these check-ins to ensure they happen consistently (or happen at all). It's also imperative that these check-ins also touch on the *positive* aspects of your relationship in addition to concerns.

Specialists strongly recommend that each of you share something positive about the other during these sessions to help make these check-ins less like an argument and more about the two of you working together for a common goal. Remember, if you want to set aside time for them, then you surely love them. Make sure you find positives about them and your relationship before engaging in a check-in. After you hype each other up and communicate your appreciation for one another, it is then time to open the floor for all honesty. This will allow you to address areas of improvement and actively work together to adjust your relationship. Make sure that you are open to feedback and be ready to make changes and sacrifices for the sake of your relationship.

Pick a Regular Time

Ideally, you'll both be relaxed, present, and in a good mood, so don't schedule a check-in after a long day at work or when you're short of time. You want to bring your best attitude and a clear mindset to these meetings with your partner.

Set the Scene

Your relationship check-in is an opportunity to slow down and connect, so why not make it feel a little special? To that end, bring your favorite snacks and drinks—and conduct the check-in somewhere that feels good to both of you. It needs to be a private and secluded atmosphere, so you both feel comfortable getting real. Ordering takeout and planning something relaxing to do afterward can also help set the mood and feel like a great reward or incentive.

However, do keep in mind that it is encouraged to have these conversations without the influence of alcohol.

Set a Time Limit

You don't want this to become a huge time sink, and you never want it to feel like a chore, so aim for a manageable timescale, especially in the beginning. These check-ins are about opening the lines of communication in a safe and calm manner; you might not resolve everything all at once. Rather, it allows you to create healthy boundaries when expressing vulnerabilities in every facet of your relationship.

Celebrate and Appreciate Each Other

Always start with the positives of your relationship. This appreciation helps each partner remember why they're doing all of this in the first place! Giving compliments and joyful feedback upfront helps your partner feel comfortable and valued. This is especially necessary if there are more challenging topics to discuss afterward. Appreciation and validation are essential ingredients for a quality relationship.

Always Finish on a High Point

A celebration, even a small one, can be a fun way to wrap up the check-in. Remember, these check-ins aren't meant to regurgitate everything your partner has done wrong since your last check-in. You should be having conversations about issues or wrongdoings as they happen. This is merely a time to check in on how everyone is doing and if there are still adjustments to be made. If you wait to vent during these check-ins, and these check-ins alone, you may be a powder keg next to an open flame—ready to explode!

Also, remember to end the session with a physical touch or an affirmation. Even if things get a little tense or something feels unresolved, find a way to come back to each other and your overall belief in the relationship. If you're checking in regularly and discussing action items as they crop up, it's clear that your relationship is worth believing in.

How to Check in with Friends or Other Family Members

Start simple. Send a text or make a phone call. They don't have to be grand or time-consuming. However, if you would like something a little more intimate, ask them out for coffee or lunch. Whichever sort of format you choose, make sure you:

- **Are prepared to be vulnerable**: Sharing with your friend is an incredibly powerful experience and is truly beneficial to the relationship, but it can also be a little more difficult to be vulnerable with a friend or other family member than it is with your partner. Be prepared to be vulnerable if necessary.

- **Can be confidential:** Remember that trust is critical in any relationship. No one tells you something in confidence that they want you to spread around. Make sure that you're willing to keep the conversation between you and your friend if you're going to let them tell you anything of merit.

- **Know that you don't have to fix the issue:** No one is expecting you to wave a magic wand and fix everything that is going wrong in your friend's life. Most of the time, your loved one doesn't even want you to. Most of the time, they just want a friendly shoulder to lean on and a pair of listening ears.

Make sure that if you haven't seen each other in a while, whether it's defined as a regular emotional check-in or not, you meet somewhere private so as to not be distracted or disturbed.

Know and Communicate Your Limits

The ability to recognize your pain or distress requires that you embrace your limits. This goes along with self-care, expressing yourself, reflecting on yourself, finding out what makes you "tick," and setting appropriate boundaries. It all builds on one another. Each of us has inherent limits, as well as personal limits, that are rooted in our own personalities.

For example, one obvious limit is that everyone needs sleep on a regular and consistent basis. However, there are less obvious ones such as "playtime". We have all heard the saying "work hard, play hard," and this is true. We work hard every day—and we do need to play hard, too. This "play" is the time of leisure that every person does need a bit of for mental health. We need to spend time doing things that bring us joy to prevent burnout and depression. The amount of "playtime" depends on the person. Know your limits with this. Your mental health will thank you.

Other examples may include the amount of money you need in your savings account in order to feel prepared for emergencies, as well as your tolerance for certain things (outspoken and angry people, slow drivers, the patience you have for slow drivers, screaming babies, etc.—it's all fair game).

However, although we all have our limits, some people have a difficult time accepting it. There is almost a desire to have no limits, which stems from confusing them with weakness. Still, if you recognize that everyone has limits and find your own, you can more easily notice when you have pushed beyond them. This allows for validation of our own emotions and therefore the opportunity to learn to regulate by taking a step back from whatever is overstimulating us and refocusing on what it is that we need to do. For example, if you have a highly demanding position at work and have loads and loads of paperwork to finish and never take a break, it is completely valid to be exhausted and frustrated. By understanding your own emotional distress, you are able to also learn more compassion so that you can notice when others have reached their limits as well.

Key Takeaways

In "Chapter 2: Communication with Yourself and Others," you are offered a little insight into nurturing your relationship with others. This is achieved by promoting your emotional well-being and filling you with compassion and care—for yourself and others. Chapter 2 emphasizes the crucial role of effective communication, highlighting not only verbal expression but also the significance of body language and being aware of your tone when you communicate.

Cultivating compassion and empathy—and being able to distinguish between the two—can also be a great result formed from proper communication. Truly understanding others as well as their perspectives can only be achieved when appropriate listening skills are met.

This chapter also discusses the need to leave the past in the past and offers advice to forgive and accept what has happened in an effort to move forward and flourish with a healthy mindset. Strategies for moving forward include focusing on the present, acknowledging your own emotions and traumas, and seeking professional help if needed.

The guide also delves into the importance of setting and respecting boundaries in all relationships. Everyone has boundaries, and it is noted not to confuse them with selfishness but rather to see them as love—for yourself and for others. The chapter advocates for the practice of saying "no" when necessary in an effort to prioritize self-care.

And speaking of self-care, regular emotional check-ins are not only for others but also for yourself. While it is necessary to check in with others as part of proper communication, providing self-care to yourself begins with emotional check-ins. It is a time set aside in which you can reflect on how you are doing—truly. This is also a great opportunity to recognize your limits so that you can best communicate them with others. By acknowledging your own boundaries and needs, you can foster greater understanding and acceptance of yourself, and by taking care of your needs, your mental health will thank you.

Chapter 3

Appreciate Your Family and Friends—and Yourself

In the journey of life, our relationships are the very fabric of our existence. They shape our experiences and emotions, and because of that, our relationships shape our overall well-being. It is important to nurture positive connections to not only enrich our lives but also strengthen our resilience by growing a positive support system. In this chapter, we delve into the essential components of cultivating meaningful relationships, from prioritizing rest and relaxation with loved ones to embarking on exciting adventures together.

Nurture Positive Relationships

Nurturing positive and healthy relationships is paramount for overall well-being and fulfillment in life. These relationships serve as the foundation upon which we build our support systems, experience love and belonging, and find companionship and understanding. Here are several key reasons why nurturing such relationships is crucial:

- **Emotional support:** Positive relationships provide a safe space for us to express our thoughts, feelings, and vulnerabilities without fear of being judged. Having someone to confide in during challenging times can significantly reduce stress and anxiety levels and also help you feel secure and safe.

- **Sense of belonging:** Healthy relationships—specifically with family and close friends—allow for a sense of belonging merely by having a deep connection with others. Knowing that we are valued and accepted for who we are allows us to develop a deep sense of identity and purpose, contributing to overall happiness and fulfillment.

- **Improved mental health:** Research consistently shows that strong social connections are linked to better mental health outcomes. Positive relationships can act as a buffer against depression, anxiety, and loneliness, which in turn provides emotional stability and support during difficult times.

- **Enhanced physical health:** Beyond mental well-being, nurturing positive relationships can also have tangible benefits for physical health. Studies have demonstrated that those with strong social support networks tend to have lower rates of chronic illness, faster recovery times from illness or surgery, and even increased longevity. This is likely due to a link between physical and mental health and well-being.

- **Personal growth:** Healthy relationships provide opportunities for personal growth and self-discovery. Through positive interactions with others (beginning in infancy), we learn valuable communication skills, empathy, and conflict resolution skills. Additionally, supportive relationships encourage us to pursue our goals and aspirations by providing encouragement and motivation along the way.

- **Happiness and fulfillment:** We can't forget happiness. It is likely the most important benefit of all. Positive relationships contribute to overall happiness and life satisfaction. Sharing meaningful experiences, creating lasting memories, and experiencing mutual growth and development with loved ones are some of the most rewarding aspects of human connection—and life in general.

Avoid Toxic Relationships

Many people experience toxic relationships at one point or another. It may be a friend who you learn talks behind your back—or maybe it's a relationship with someone who cheats on you. No matter the degree of toxicity, these relationships can be damaging to emotional health.

To avoid a toxic relationship, it's first critical to understand warning signs. Signs such as someone showing a lack of respect, being overly negative consistently, or being possessive or controlling are often indicators of toxicity. Having personal boundaries—just like discussed earlier in this guide—can help avoid some of these behaviors on the front end. However, if something seems off in a relationship—no matter if it's a friendship, familial relationship, or partnership—it may be a sign to take a step back and assess.

Seek relationships that promote mutual respect, support, and growth, and avoid those that are draining to your mental or physical well-being. You can do this by properly spending time to understand your own values and what you seek in your relationship.

Assessing a Relationship for Toxicity

When trying to pinpoint a toxic relationship, it may be easiest to look into the impact the relationship has on you and your well-being. To do this, it is essential to trust your gut reactions and pay close attention to how you feel when you are with specific people.

Asking yourself questions and reviewing your answers is one of the easiest ways to tell if someone is healthy or unhealthy for you. It is important to note that a relationship can be toxic without the other person being a bad person. Sometimes, we just aren't compatible, and our mental health diminishes around these people. Whatever the case, make sure you're assessing your relationships with the following questions:

- How do I feel when this person is around?

- Am I the best version of myself in their company?

- Do I feel safe with this person (to express my feelings or emotions, as well as physically safe)?

- When I'm not with them, how do I feel?

The truth of the matter is, if being with a specific friend, family member, or partner makes you feel inadequate, discouraged, stupid, ashamed, or unsafe, they are—or the relationship is—toxic, and it's causing trauma to your life. It is important to know that some people will bring out the best in us—and likewise, some can bring out the absolute worst.

How to Leave a Toxic Relationship

As is everything in this guide, this pertains to more than merely romantic relationships. All of our relationships matter in our lifetime. Relationships such as friendships, familial relationships, and romantic partnerships can all equally be toxic. So how do you leave a toxic relationship?

Build a Safety Net

This is the first step in ridding yourself of toxic people or relationships. Make a plan for how you are going to deal with the transition. If the relationship is a romantic partner that you live with, make sure you have a plan about where you're going to stay when you leave and what you will take with you. If it's a family member, make a plan on how you might avoid them for family gatherings or family-related events. If it's a friend and you share a friend circle, make a plan for that as well.

Surround Yourself with Positive Friends and Family

Your friends and family are most often there to support you—let them. Once you decide to leave a relationship, especially if there is a safety concern, these are the people who can be there for you every step of the way. They can give you courage and show you what life can look like outside of this relationship. Communicate with them and let them know what's going on. Let them help you.

Healing from Unhealthy Relationships

So, you left a toxic relationship. That wasn't easy. But now, perhaps, comes the more difficult part—healing. Toxic relationships are harmful to everyone involved and can cause long-lasting damage, like severe trauma. Even after leaving the relationship behind, it's natural to still have the same emotions you had before leaving them. You may even be traumatized into believing you need the relationship to move forward. You don't.

Oftentimes, trauma-filled relationships hardwire your brain differently, similarly to a drug, which leaves you feeling dependent on the drug. The truth is the pain this type of relationship can cause can lead to depression and anxiety—with or without them nearby. It may damage your self-esteem and self-worth. The chronic emotional and mental stress of being surrounded by toxicity can take a toll on your mental health.

Work with your support group, and seek professional health to move forward if you ever:

- Feel like you need the relationship again

- Are responding to your trauma in unhealthy ways

- Are depressed

Keep Commitments

Commitments are thrown at us from any and all angles throughout our lifetime. In fact, the foundation of civil society is the belief that—generally speaking—people will usually keep their word and fulfill their obligations.

Moral development research doesn't address making and keeping promises, but many would say that your moral compass would be rooted in your ability to do so. In fact, there is quite the psychological weight behind promises.

Promises seem to keep us bonded with each other. From marriage vows to work deadlines, promises tend to be part of our everyday human interaction. A promise is simply an intention statement, a social construct that says, "Because I said I will, I will."

By making a commitment, we show cooperation as well as reliability, which are essential traits for establishing and preserving solid bonds with others. But more than that, our sense of self is significantly impacted by promises as well. Integrity and self-worth are based on our ability to keep our word. According to research, keeping your word opens up reward regions in the brain, which elevates your mood and sense of value. Plus, others start to see you as trustworthy.

Impact of Broken Promises

Sometimes, even with our best intentions in mind, promises aren't always kept. There could be serious repercussions if this happens. When promises are broken, its impact can be seen on relationships, which can be weakened. When it comes to relationships, trust is everything—and if you break promises, especially several, trust can be lost. Other emotions, such as disappointment and resentment, can also become prevalent, which makes it very difficult to mend the brokenness of the relationship.

Overall, the nature of a commitment, the motivations behind breaking one, along with the dynamics of the relationships you have with the other person all affect how severe the consequences can be. For example, not showing up to a basketball game for your child isn't as detrimental to them and your relationship as missing their graduation. Likewise, breaking a promise to your spouse to fix something around the house is not quite as severe as breaking the promise of your marriage vows and cheating. There are different levels of breaking promises, and consequences that follow are likely going to mirror the level of "betrayal."

However, try to refrain from overpromising. Offer what is manageable and attainable in manageable steps, and avoid getting ahead of yourself. Make an honest assessment of your abilities and limitations, taking into account any practical obstacles to your job, health, finances, or other obligations. Even if you really want to do something and care deeply about the situation at hand, there might be a possibility that you have to say no—or, at the very least, avoid making a promise.

Treat Loved Ones to R&R

Long-term stress, if left untreated and simply ignored, can cause chest pain, headaches, digestive issues, anxiety, depression, changes in sexual desire and inability to focus. It may not seem like a big deal to skip relaxation in your daily routine. But it is.

A little R&R can go a long way in:

- Reducing stress and anxiety

- Improving mood

- Decreasing blood pressure

- Chronic pain relief

- Improving immune health

- Stronger cardiovascular system

In the hustle and bustle of everyday life, it's easy to get caught up in the whirlwind of the world and the responsibilities and commitments that come from it. We often even neglect our own well-being, and at times, we also neglect the needs of our loved ones.

However, prioritizing rest and relaxation—both for ourselves and our loved ones—is essential for growing and maintaining healthy, fulfilling relationships. People love feeling special and pampered—so treat yourself and your loved ones to some good ol' fashioned R&R.

For Family and Friends

Taking time out to rest and relax with our family and friends is not only enjoyable but also great for strengthening our bonds with them. They feel appreciated, pampered, and this rest and relaxation you offer can really aid in their mental health, which, in turn, gives them more energy for relationships—including the one they share with you. Whether it's a cozy movie night at home, a leisurely hike in nature, a full-blown spa day, or a relaxing day at the beach, carving out dedicated time for shared leisure activities can be an enjoyable way to spend time with family and friends.

For Yourself

In addition to nurturing relationships with our family and friends, it's equally important to prioritize our own self-care and well-being, which is a common theme in this guide on 50 Ways to Love Your Life. Here are some ways to incorporate rest and relaxation into your own life:

- **Schedule regular "you time":** Carve out dedicated time in your schedule for self-care activities that help you relax and recharge. This can be reading a book, taking a nice, hot bubble bath, meditating/praying, or going to get your hair cut or to enjoy a massage. Whatever you do, prioritize yourself and your own relaxation. This will rejuvenate you and give you the ability to tackle whatever is to come next with a newfound energy. Whatever you do, just make sure that you're kind to yourself—especially during times of stress or difficulty. Treat yourself with the same love and understanding that you would offer to a close friend, and remember that it's okay to take breaks and prioritize your own well-being.

- **Engage in activities that bring you joy:** Make time for activities that bring you joy and fulfillment, whether it's pursuing a creative hobby, spending time in nature, or simply indulging in your favorite pastimes. By prioritizing activities that nourish your soul and bring you happiness, you'll enhance your overall quality of life and deepen your sense of contentment. This is often the best kind of rest and relaxation.

Rest and Relaxation Tips

Make Time

We make time every day to eat, run errands, take our kids to school and appointments, etc.—why should rest be any different? Find what relaxation technique works for you to determine how much time you'll need, and set aside time every week to make it happen! This could be those activities you enjoy, listening to music, spa day, nail salon, day at the beach, walking in nature, reading a book, taking a bath—whatever! Just make sure you find something you enjoy, make time to do it, and make it consistent enough that you can feel refreshed.

Get Enough Sleep

In addition to rest and relaxation, it's recommended that adults get seven to eight hours of sleep each night, but understand that quality sleep is just as important as the number of hours. Rapid eye movement (REM) sleep is the most restorative of the five sleep cycles. At least one-quarter of your sleep should be spent in the REM cycle, and there are a few ways to ensure that you get enough of that:

- Avoiding caffeine later in the day

- Sticking to a consistent sleep schedule, even on vacations and weekends

- Setting your thermostat between 60 to 70 degrees F each night

- Limiting screen time, especially at night

- Avoiding working out later in the day

- Doing something relaxing right before bed

Plan an Adventure

Adventure makes life a little more worthwhile. There's the thrill of planning, the excitement of the unknown, the freedom of not having a schedule and relying on joy and excitement to drive you.

The "adventure mindset" is something that psychologists recommend when you feel your life needs a little spicing up. Treat life as the adventure it is. It is an exercise that is especially fun with your friends and family and can truly show your appreciation and love for them by including them. Whether it be planning surprising or adventurous events, getaways, or trying new and exhilarating foods and hobbies—make sure that you keep that "adventure mindset" to ensure that you're seeking a thrill at every turn!

Surprise Party

Something that most people enjoy is surprises! Treat your family and friends to a surprise party for a little extra adventure and excitement.

Adventure Getaway

Surprise them with an adventurous weekend getaway. Choose destinations that offer thrilling experiences like hiking a rigorous trail, zip-lining, rock-climbing wall, exploring a new city, and if they are particularly adventurous—add in a helicopter ride or something equally as thrilling! Extroverts often find excitement in new and dynamic environments, but there are plenty of adventure getaways for the more introverted friends and family members.

The stair-stepping adventure list is another great fun activity to do with your family and friends if they're particularly interested in seeking thrill and excitement. The idea is when you master one thing, see if they want to try something new—one step up. For example:

- If they have tried sledding, have them try snowboarding or skiing.

- If they have tried a Ferris wheel, have them try a roller coaster.

- If they have tried a ropes course, have them try zip-lining.

- If they have tried the monkey bars, have them try climbing a tree.

- If they have tried biking, have them try mountain biking.

- If they have tried skateboarding on the sidewalk, have them try skateboarding at the skate park.

- If they tried canoeing or kayaking, have them try river rafting.

Keep the family dynamics fresh and exciting by occasionally stepping out of comfort zones and encouraging everyone else to do the same. Trying new things together can be an adventure that strengthens the bond you all have. Whether it's taking a dance class, exploring a new hiking trail, or attending an art exhibit, your family and friends will definitely appreciate your efforts in breaking up the monotony.

After all, life is all about adventures. Trying new things and embracing the fact that we are all unique individuals with our own interests will make your lives together go a lot more smoothly. It can even make it that much more exciting and adventurous. Just make sure you celebrate your loved ones' passions and encourage them in all of your endeavors together.

Experience New Hobbies

Journeying through life is all about exploration. Discovering and trying new things is a chance to find new passions. This can also be an effective way to grow relationships too! After all, the key to keeping a strong connection with your loved ones is to continually grow—with them. What better way to bring forth some freshness than to find a fun new hobby you can partake in with them?

When exploring new activities to try, consider their interests and preferences as well as your own. You can take turns choosing activities with them, ensuring that you each have a say. Be open to trying things you may not have considered before; you might come to find that you enjoy something you never thought you could.

Whether it's trying a new cuisine, taking up a dance class, embarking on a road trip, or learning a new skill, the key is to approach these experiences with an open heart and mind and be willing to embrace the unknown. Know that at the end of the day, even if you don't enjoy the activity, you're doing something different that is sure to create memories and strengthen who you are—and the relationship with the person you may be experiencing these things with, by just spending quality time together.

Keep in mind that everyone may enjoy different activities, but it's important for you to try things even if you don't think you would enjoy them. You might surprise yourself!

Travel Somewhere New

Plan and take trips! By yourself, with a friend, with a partner—it doesn't matter. Just go. Make sure you're exploring new places, cultures, and cuisines since this is what life is all about! In fact, human beings have traveled for centuries. Exploration is almost ingrained in us thickly like an instinct. Historically, travel started out as a purely practical instinct. We traveled for food, better environments, etc. As civilization began to grow, it was mostly done for the purpose of profit and power. Merchants sailed on long journeys to sell their wares and exchange their items for goods needed back home. We exchanged cultures and knowledge throughout different parts of the world with others, and eventually, we got to where we are now—traveling for fun. Traveling is far easier these days, whether it's in a car, a boat, a plane, a helicopter, a train—it doesn't matter. You can go almost anywhere your heart desires.

So where does your heart desire to go?

Health Benefits

Travel can improve both our physical and mental health. Studies have shown that vacations can reduce stress and the potential for burnout, as well as just genuinely make people happier and healthier. Traveling has been found to increase creativity and appreciation for other cultures and sights, which makes our brains more alert by keeping them active. It also gives us even more opportunities to socialize, grow, and expand our minds to differences that others may have in other areas of the world.

Emotional Wellness

Vacationing in new places improves emotional agility because it exposes you to completely new experiences and sometimes cultures. Our emotional agility is our ability to deal with and express emotions. It can help us to adapt and react better to unforeseen situations and problems by slowing down and evaluating situations before making abrupt decisions. This is due to our improved sense of empathy and perspective from learning how different people around the world live, think, and view the world. These experiences can truly help us to interact more understandingly and appreciatively with people in our daily lives.

New Experiences Lead to Better Brain Function

People often seek new knowledge and experiences naturally. As human beings, we learn to love. Our perception of the world changes and expands as we meet new people, see new places, and learn about different cultures and parts of the world. When our usual routine changes, our brains experience new things, which also improves our cognitive abilities. As we learn and shift our brains to adjust to new streets, surroundings, words, and overall new ways of doing things, we stimulate neuroplasticity and improve our brain health, memory, and learning abilities.

Self-Discovery

Traveling allows us to learn more about ourselves and improves our self-confidence. As we go through new experiences and deal with unexpected situations, we learn more about our own character, how we deal with good and bad things in life, and how we can improve from here. We also learn that we are stronger and more resilient than we think when we finally get out of our own comfort zones, challenge ourselves, and deal with the difficulties that we come across on our journeys.

Nostalgia

The joy of traveling can be found not only in new experiences but also in old ones. We've all been to a museum or a particular town that we've wanted to go back to. Our memories of those places make us want to revisit and reexperience the happiness and excitement we felt when we went the first time, so we can harness a sense of nostalgia by incorporating old travels into our present and remind ourselves of another time. In fact, over time, our connection to the places we visit strengthens, and they become part of us and our history. Revisiting them is actually great for your psyche.

Traveling is an incredibly enjoyable pastime, whether we do it alone or with our loved ones. It's something everyone can learn to appreciate, and the more you go and experience other worlds, the more you realize that you will begin to anticipate the next journey, whether it's a thrilling adventure or a relaxing stay at a beach resort.

So, while you eagerly await the next trip, take time to appreciate the reasons we enjoy these experiences by remembering that our enjoyment goes beyond just the positive feelings—it resides in our overall health. Traveling improves the very way we function, both mentally and physically. Through travel, we develop, grow, and become better people and better members of society—and likely better partners, friends, and family members.

Cherish Memories

Revisiting cherished memories and reliving special moments can be a powerful way to enhance emotional closeness with people. Remember, it doesn't take long to develop lasting memories with someone. So whether you have been friends with someone all your life or it's just a recent development, it's possible that you have great memories together. Not to mention your memories with your loved ones (those who are only in the past and those in the present), and it's often necessary to take a little walk down memory lane by:

- **Looking at photos:** These photos can be from your childhood or even more recent.

- **Creating a memory jar:** This is a fun activity, no matter your age. You can do this with a friend or family member, too, to make it extra fun and engaging! Each of you should write down your favorite memories together on small sheets of paper and place them in a jar. Go through them periodically together, especially when you're looking at shedding some positivity on the friendship.

- **Revisiting special places:** These can be places special to you specifically or one you share with others. These can consist of:

  - Favorite vacation spots

  - The place where you first met your significant other

  - Your childhood hometown

  - A special restaurant you have visited

  - A favorite theme park

- **Watching home movies:** Pull out old videos of your life. This can be on a disc, a VHS, or even in digital format. It is recommended to broadcast it to a large screen, if possible, if you're doing this with loved ones, but regardless, make it a nice experience. Create a comfortable sitting environment and get out the popcorn and candy! Have fun with it!

Connect Deeply with Others

Establishing meaningful connections with others goes beyond surface-level interactions. It's all about trust, empathy, and understanding with those around you, whether in your personal or professional life. But how do you move past casual conversations and create genuine relationships?

Be Curious

Genuine interest in others can be a powerful bonding tool. People can read when you're truly interested in them and curious about what it is that makes them unique. Ask open-ended questions that encourage them to share their thoughts, experiences, and aspirations. Listen attentively (use active listening skills discussed in Chapter 2) without judgment, and respond thoughtfully to demonstrate your engagement.

Be Vulnerable

Being vulnerable isn't easy. We can all agree with that, and it's likely the last thing you want to do with someone you just met. However, it is critical to form deep and meaningful connections. Share your own stories, fears, dreams, and all the emotions in between to create a space for openness and trust. However, be mindful of boundaries—theirs and yours—and avoid oversharing, especially in the early stages of interaction. Don't be afraid to trust people, but it is a balancing act. You don't want to misplace your trust.

Be Empathetic

Empathy allows you to understand and connect with others on an emotional level. It's the opportunity to truly put yourself in their shoes, acknowledge their feelings, and offer support without judgment. Avoid giving unsolicited advice and focus on validating their experiences. By being empathetic toward someone you want to deepen your relationship, you open up the door for them to feel validated and understood.

Be Respectful

Respect forms the basis of all healthy relationships. Treat others with kindness, courtesy, and dignity, respect and honor their boundaries, limitations, and preferences, and they will immediately look at you in a positive light. Maintain positive communication and avoid behaviors like gossiping or mocking, and you will show your integrity and character to others, which is the foundation of all deep connections—trust.

Be Generous

Generosity shows goodwill and appreciation in a relationship. By offering your time, resources, or support to help others, you can help them achieve their goals and overcome challenges, which opens the door to love and admiration. Celebrate their achievements, express gratitude for their contributions, and help them as often as you can. Remember, though, relationships are two-way streets. Never allow your generosity to be taken for granted. Don't be generous in hopes of a return—but don't become a doormat either.

Be Consistent

Consistency is key to building trust and reliability in relationships. Follow through on your commitments, check in regularly (with relationship check-ins and just regular "how are you doing" check-ins), and show consistent support in both good and bad times, and you will certainly be able to cultivate a deeper connection with whomever you wish!

Show You Care with Surprises

Think of how your loved ones show happiness or something that genuinely makes them happy. Think about their personality type and think of ideas of how you might surprise them. One loved one might love a surprise trip or experience out, but another might prefer a nice gift and a quiet evening at home. Think about what your loved one does for fun, and you'll have a great idea of how to surprise them!

There are multiple ways you can surprise your loved ones, and this may be in the form of a gift, an outing, or just spending quality time together. Figure out what they need or even just want. Is there a special treat they enjoy that they haven't had in a while? Are they super stressed and could benefit from a spa day? Try to plan a surprise that's related to their hobbies or needs. If their favorite band is coming to town, consider buying tickets so that the two of you can go to the concert together. If they've had a tough day at work and you know they have a sweet tooth, go get a box of cookies and enjoy them together while you binge-watch your favorite show. Whatever the case, cater it to your friend and surprise them! It doesn't have to be grand! Just make sure it's something they enjoy! This can really deepen the connection the two of you have, and oftentimes, the work you put into relationships reaps rewards. Ultimately, isn't showing people you care and them showing they care what life is all about?

Key Takeaways

"Chapter 3: Appreciate Your Family and Your Friends—and Yourself" is all about just that. Appreciating others—and yourself. Nurturing positive relationships and prioritizing rest, relaxation, and adventure are essential for a fulfilling and healthy life. Positive relationships are often seen as your "support network" and offer emotional support, provide a sense of belonging, and facilitate personal growth. On the other hand, toxic relationships can harm mental and physical health quickly. Steer clear of those who are toxic, and work to rid yourself of a relationship that has become toxic. Rely on a safety net with friends and family, have a plan, and once you are free, make sure that you take the proper care to heal completely. Feelings of depression, low self-esteem, and fear and anxiety are all natural, but it may require speaking to a mental health professional to fully heal from prolonged trauma.

Rest and relaxation practices are essential. Treat your family and friends to R&R, too, because that time to disengage from the rest of the world will rejuvenate them just as much as it will you, giving everyone more battery power for later. "You time" should be scheduled just as everything else is in our busy lives, and in doing so—and setting appropriate boundaries in addition—can help reduce stress and promote overall well-being.

Engaging in leisure activities with loved ones is another way to appreciate them—and yourself—as it grows bonds and creates lasting memories. Beyond that, keeping the excitement alive by maintaining an "adventure mindset" is also great for your relationships. Adventure encourages physical fitness, mental resilience, and natural exhilaration, all of which enrich your life experiences. By exploring new hobbies, traveling, and cherishing memories along the way, you are able to keep an active and healthy lifestyle worthy of appreciation and, in doing so, have the opportunity to truly deepen the connections you have with others.

Remember, emotional closeness and lasting bonds are what life is all about. Surprising loved ones with thoughtful gestures tailored to their interests further strengthens relationships, validating them for who they are, establishing that care and appreciation you're hoping to share, and enhancing overall happiness and fulfillment.

Chapter 4

Keep Yourself Healthy

Our overall health is a myriad of threads woven together. It's complex and multi-faceted since it encompasses quite literally every aspect of our existence. Our mental, physical, and emotional health all play a huge role in our overall health, and each and every experience, person, or event in our lives can have an effect. From the bonds we share with friends to the diligence with which we care for our bodies, every choice we make contributes to the overall fabric of our health and happiness. In this chapter, we embark on a journey through the realms of holistic well-being, exploring the diverse practices and habits that can enrich our lives and nurture our spirits (spiritual health is also a major proponent of mental health). From the joy of shared activities to the importance of regular health checkups, from the nourishment of nutritious foods to the rejuvenation of restful sleep, we lightly touch on all the ways in which we can cultivate vitality and resilience. By embracing these principles, we can craft a richer, more vibrant existence—one filled with vitality, purpose, and fulfillment. So, to discover more of the *50 Ways to Love Your Life*, let's venture into how to keep yourself as healthy as humanly possible.

Do Activities You Enjoy

As adults, we all have hobbies, and there may be some that you already enjoy participating in, whether it be by yourself or with loved ones. However, exploring brand-new activities or hobbies can be an exciting way to enjoy life and socialize and grow bonds with our loved ones. It creates memories, and you begin to associate this fun and new experience with your friend, which can truly strengthen your relationship together.

Whether it's learning a new skill, embarking on a creative project together, or engaging in a shared interest that neither of you has tried before, it can really improve your connection with them.

Some hobbies you might consider are:

- **Cooking or Baking:** Experimenting with new recipes or baking homemade treats that you saw online or on TV can be fun and delicious.

- **Gardening:** Gardening is not only a relaxing hobby but can also lead to beautiful results.

- **Painting or Drawing:** Explore your artistic side by taking up painting, drawing, or other forms of visual art. You can create your own art or attend art classes. Now, there are even "painting with a twist" classes that involve wine and other fun elements.

- **Hiking or Nature Walks:** Enjoy the great outdoors by going on hikes or nature walks in local parks or nature reserves. It's an excellent way to stay active and appreciate nature.

- **Photography:** Capture moments and memories by taking up photography. You can explore your surroundings and document your adventures together.

- **Playing Musical Instruments:** Learning a new instrument together can be difficult but also incredibly rewarding. Consider taking joint classes and jamming together!

- **Bird-watching:** Bird-watching can be a relaxing and educational hobby. Get a pair of binoculars and observe the various bird species in your area. Put up a few feeders nearby and enjoy them up close, as well.

- **Knitting:** Learning how to make your own garments or blankets can be fun and can give you and your friend a chance to catch up and talk while you make them!

- **Wine or Beer Tasting:** If you're of legal drinking age and appreciate beer or wine, you can explore different wineries or breweries together.

- **Puzzle Solving:** Work on jigsaw puzzles, crosswords, or brain-teasers together. Puzzle solving can be a mentally stimulating and enjoyable pastime. There are subscription boxes you can sign up for, too, and make it a monthly ritual to solve a new one together!

- **Dancing:** Learn different dance styles like ballroom, salsa, or swing dancing. You can take classes or learn from

YouTube.

- **Book Club:** Start a book club and read and discuss books together. It's an excellent way to share your thoughts and insights on various literature—and this can even open up the door to more in-depth and meaningful discussions.

- **Yoga or Meditation:** We discussed that self-care is important, and yoga and meditation is a great two-for-one. You can practice self-care and participate in great quality time with your friend if you do it together! Use it as a way to stay healthy and reduce stress, and if you want to make it extra fun, attend a class together.

- **Volunteer Work:** Find a cause or organization each of you are passionate about and sign up to volunteer. It's a meaningful way to give back to the community together.

- **Stargazing:** Bring the chairs and the snacks and spend evenings stargazing and identifying constellations. Consider investing in a telescope for more in-depth celestial exploration and keep track of events happening in your viewing area.

- **Model Car Building:** Pick up an old craft like building model cars! It's possible this can hold some nostalgia behind it, but if either of you is a car fan, definitely consider this as a fun, engaging, and satisfying option.

- **Home Improvement:** Collaborate on home improvement projects or DIY renovations. This can be a productive and satisfying way to upgrade your living space.

Branch out, too, and potentially earn extra cash in the meantime.

- **Travel:** Plan and take trips together. Make sure you're exploring new places, cultures, and cuisines since this is all about trying new things together and truly experiencing things with one another. Traveling can create unforgettable shared experiences.

Remember that the key to a successful shared hobby is to choose activities that all parties can enjoy and that align with everyone's interests and abilities. But really, make sure that whatever you and your friend choose, you're able to experience it for the first time together and that you stay consistent and keep at it!

Go to the Doctor Regularly

It doesn't matter what stage of life you are in. You could be a fresh young adult, the parent of young children, an empty nester, or somewhere in between all of that—but the truth is that it doesn't matter. No matter how old you are, it is imperative to visit your family doctor frequently.

There is evidence that shows regular doctor visits can save you both time (because you won't be sick as much during the year) and money (because you won't be paying for large problems that were left untreated). Here are some reason great benefits of going to routine doctor visits:

- **Significantly lower health care costs:** Heading into a doctor's office for a regular checkup is relatively cheap and, with insurance, can even be free. However, even without insurance, a regular checkup can still be one of the most cost-effective health services you can have. Regular checkups can eliminate the risk of major health problems developing (because checkups aid in preventive care and also allow for early detection of issues), which can both be life-threatening and costly. In some cases, having a regular checkup with your family doctor can help you avoid surgery, medication, or other procedures that can add up quickly.

- **Kill disease early:** It's no secret that the longer a disease or illness has to fester in your body, the worse it can get. Regular checkups with a doctor can help detect and diagnose ailments before they spread or turn into a more serious condition.

- **Identify disorders:** Even if you feel perfectly healthy, there is a good chance that you aren't! This is especially true if you have a stress-related disorder. Oftentimes, significant stress in your life can instigate a variety of health-related issues such as hypertension, high blood pressure, weight gain, mental disorders (depression, anxiety), and even digestive problems. Having a regular checkup can help diagnose these issues before they turn serious.

- **Keep yourself informed and in control:** When it comes to health, you are in control if you seek regular checkups and stay on top of your health needs. You should always drive your body every day to be healthy, but you have the choice: drive your body to be healthy or drive it to be sick. It's all based on the choices you make. What you eat, how you exercise (or if you exercise), whether you go to the doctor or not, and what you do to take care of your mental health—it all plays into how well your body will perform. Taking time for regular checkups with family physicians or a doctor can help you stay informed about your health and help you make important decisions for years to come.

Eat Nutritious Foods and Hydrate

Good nutrition and hydration are important at any age. Maintaining a healthy diet and staying properly hydrated can help you increase your energy levels, control your weight, and may even prevent certain health problems from rearing their ugly heads. Diseases such as heart disease, high blood pressure, type 2 diabetes, and osteoporosis are some of the biggest names that can quite easily be prevented with a well-orchestrated plan between you and your doctor when it comes to your nutrition.

Understanding what a well-balanced diet looks like is vital for staying healthy throughout your life. What we eat plays a large role in how we feel, regardless of our age. Our bodies rely on macronutrients, which are the proteins, carbohydrates, and healthy fats in food for fuel and energy to get through each and every day. In order for our bodies to thrive, all of our necessary nutrients must be replaced daily. It is also important to ensure you're getting enough micronutrients, such as vitamins and minerals, to sustain the lifestyle you wish.

Most of us know that proper nutrition and diet can help maintain a healthy weight, but there are many other benefits as well, such as living longer, having a lower risk of chronic diseases (heart disease and diabetes, for example), and lowering your risk for cold and flu every year.

Signs of Inadequate Nutrition and Dehydration

Nutrient deficiencies and malnutrition can lead to a variety of health concerns, such as:

- Unexplained fatigue
- Getting sick often
- Bruised or dry, cracked skin
- Wounds that are slow to heal
- Ridged or spoon-shaped nails
- Trouble chewing or swallowing
- Loss of appetite
- Weight loss
- Muscle weakness

Maintain Proper Hygiene

When you think of hygiene, the first things that likely come to mind are brushing your teeth, taking a shower, washing your hands, or any daily practice to help keep your body clean and healthy. And this is true—and aside from taking care of your physical body and practicing good mental health, hygiene is equally important. Hygiene keeps your body free of bacteria, and hygiene has been shown to be directly related to both physical and mental health and well-being. Keep yourself clean. Keep yourself happy. Keep yourself well.

If that seems daunting, then chances are that you may have slacked on your own personal hygiene. While it is true that skipping these things may seem easier in the short term, it can develop into a long-term issue. Improving personal hygiene is simpler than you might think, and it doesn't have to break the bank or be a huge time sink. Making small adjustments to your daily habits little by little can have a truly significant impact. If you're unsure, consulting with a health care provider can help identify any underlying health issues.

Teeth

Start by brushing your teeth twice daily—once in the morning and again before bed—to establish a consistent routine. Just two minutes of brushing is all it takes for a thorough clean, thorough brush, and that should easily fit into your schedule, even on busy days.

Body

Daily body washing is essential. A quick shower or bath focusing on key areas like underarms and private areas is all that's needed for a quick clean. And it is even possible to hit these areas if you face a situation where water access is limited. Using a damp cloth or sponge can suffice for maintaining cleanliness.

Clothes and Bedding

Regularly laundering clothes and bedding is also crucial for hygiene maintenance. Once a week is sufficient, whether using a washing machine or washing by hand. If necessary, a quick hand wash and air dry can freshen up clothing for re-wear if you don't happen to have anything more than one set of clothing.

Handwashing

Frequent handwashing is vital to minimize the spread of certain diseases. Remember to wash your hands before and after contact with shared or potentially contaminated surfaces to protect yourself and others.

Restroom Business Hygiene

Proper wiping techniques after using the toilet are essential for cleanliness as well as odor control. Always wipe from front to back to prevent the spread of bacteria into more sensitive zones (your urethra, and in women's case, their vaginal opening). This will reduce the risk of urinary or other infections. Consider using body wipes or a bidet for added cleanliness, but they are not necessary for basic hygiene.

Hair

Hair washing should be done at least every three days, with most people not needing to shampoo daily. The frequency of washing depends on factors like hair type, sweat levels, and product usage. Aim for a balance between cleanliness and scalp health rather than focusing solely on achieving commercial-worthy hair.

Overall, maintaining good hygiene doesn't have to be complicated, expensive, or time-consuming. Simple adjustments to daily routines can make a significant difference and can be one way to aid in truly loving your life.

Meditate/Pray

Spiritual health oftentimes walks hand-in-hand with mental health. In the fast-paced rhythm of our everyday busy lives, where every moment seems to be consumed by tasks, responsibilities, and digital distractions, it's easy to lose sight of the deeper dimensions of existence. Yet, it's still important that you make time, in the midst of all the chaos, to take time for yourself and for your spiritual health—no matter what that looks like.

Somewhere, beneath all the chaos of every day, exists an oasis of serenity and spiritual nourishment. It is important that you go there and divulge in the practices of meditation or prayer. This guide is not devoted to a particular religion or denomination but instead encourages you to find some sort of spiritual solace to aid in mental clarity. Whichever belief or technique you use is completely your own.

In this section, we embark on a small journey inward, where you are encouraged to use time of rest and relaxation to find the profound benefits of finding your inner peace—whatever that looks like. For generations, the power of prayer and meditation has been spoken about. No matter what your belief, you should be able to find a bit of peace and satisfaction in establishing one of these ancient traditions to allow your spiritual self to find expression and joy. Health benefits for each are:

- **Stress reduction:** Both prayer and meditation have been found to decrease levels of the stress hormone—cortisol. This can lead to a reduction in the many negative effects of stress, including anxiety, tension, and sleep disturbances.

- **Lower blood pressure**

- **Boosted immune response**

- **Improved emotional well-being:** Regular engagement in prayer and meditation can promote feelings of peace, contentment, and happiness. These practices have been associated with better mood regulation and an overall positive emotional state.

- **Enhanced focus and concentration:** Meditation practices, especially mindfulness and concentration techniques, sharpen attention and improve cognitive control. This can lead to better decision-making and an enhanced ability to focus on tasks.

Take Care of Your Dental and Eye Care

While it may not be widely understood, there is a clear connection between a person's dental health and their mental health. While we touched upon visiting a health care professional for regular checkups and touched upon dental care in hygiene importance, it is important to note that visiting a dentist and an optometrist are also extremely helpful for your overall health.

Numerous studies have identified associations between mental health and oral health; however, the interaction often does not get much attention, even among health care professionals. Studies have shown that there are various ways in which oral health and mental health are interconnected, each having an impact on the other. Dental health problems can impact a person's quality of life and exacerbate mental health problems and vice versa.

For example:

- When a person has poor oral health, it can impact their eating, speech, and self-esteem and can even lead to reduced social interactions, which can further harm mental well-being due to feeling isolated or lonely.

- Many people, including people with mental health conditions, have anxiety associated with dental care and procedures and avoid much-needed care. Meanwhile, chronic oral pain can contribute to poor mental health. It's a cycle. And it can make treating mental health conditions more difficult.

- Symptoms of mental illnesses can contribute to poor

nutrition or hygiene, which in turn contributes to poor dental health.

- People with mental illness, particularly those experiencing symptoms of serious mental illness, may have difficulty maintaining an effective daily dental care routine and accessing needed dental treatment.

It's important to focus on your mental health as well as your dental hygiene, as the two work hand-in-hand. By going to a dentist, you can alleviate some issues and prevent larger ones from arising.

The same can be said for eye health. By going to an optometrist, you're able to prevent certain eye diseases and issues from arising or, at the very least, detect them early enough to keep them manageable. The fact is that just like declining dental health, vision loss can also affect your physical health by increasing your risk of falls and your quality of life in general, and it can also have a *huge* impact on your mental health. Loss of vision has been linked to loneliness, social isolation, and feelings of worry, anxiety, and fear. Seek out an optometrist and stay on top of your eye health!

Limit Screen Time

In this digital age, screens have become a staple in our everyday lives. It seems like we're all glued to some type of screen. From smartphones and tablets to laptops and TVs, our reliance on screens has grown exponentially over the last two decades (increasing more and more every year). While technology has undoubtedly brought numerous advantages, excessive use of screen time has also been linked to long-term health effects. And if you tack on increasing rates of social media usage in both kids and adults and the harm that can come from it, we potentially have a recipe for disaster with our long-term well-being. In fact, studies show that both physical and mental health may be improved by reducing screen time and limiting the use of social media.

Physical Health Benefits of Reducing Screen Time

- **Improved sleep quality:** Prolonged exposure to screens, especially before bedtime, has been proven to disrupt our circadian rhythm, which can make it challenging to fall asleep and stay asleep. Reducing screen time, especially in the hours leading up to the time you go to bed, can lead to improved sleep quality, leaving us more refreshed and energized the next day.

- **Reduced eye strain:** Staring at screens for extended periods can strain our eyes and lead to massive eye strain. Even with blue-light filtering glasses, it's pretty harsh on our eyes. Symptoms like dry eyes, headaches, and blurred vision can all be attributed to extended use of screens. Limiting screen time and taking regular breaks can help alleviate these discomforts and promote healthier eyesight.

- **Enhanced posture:** Excessive screen usage is associated with poor posture, often leading to shoulder, back, and, more commonly, neck pain. By reducing screen time and being mindful of our posture while using our digital devices, we can begin to mitigate musculoskeletal issues and improve our overall physical health.

Mental Health Benefits of Reducing Screen Time

- **Decreased anxiety and stress:** Constant exposure to social media and online memes and stimuli can overload your brain and contribute to anxiety and stress. Limiting screen time can help us disconnect from these triggers, allowing our minds to unwind and find peace.

- **Increased focus and productivity:** Reducing screen time can boost our ability to concentrate on tasks without all the added distractions that we are all guilty of. This heightened focus can lead to increased productivity and a greater sense of accomplishment in our daily lives.

- **Enhanced emotional well-being:** Social media, while it can be used for good, has negativity built within it. It can cause feelings of inadequacy, jealousy, and loneliness due to the constant comparison culture. Limiting your exposure to social media platforms can lead to improved emotional well-being and higher self-esteem—and help prevent the risk of cyberbullying.

Overall, reducing screen time and just being mindful of the negativity our devices can harbor truly can bring forth profound benefits for our physical and mental health. By consciously disconnecting from screens and social media, we can truly prioritize our own health and safety.

Take More Naps

As discussed a bit previously, sleep is crucial for maintaining our health. Research indicates that achieving seven to eight hours of consistent nighttime sleep is optimal for promoting good health. And although we may employ the techniques this guide offered to aid in sleep, it's still possible that a restful night's sleep eluded us the night before. So how would we combat that? How can we help our brain fog, our moodiness, our distractedness when we know it's all due to not getting enough sleep the night before?

Enter the nap.

Napping has been associated with various health benefits, including stress reduction and memory improvement. However, everyone is different. Keep in mind that naps don't affect everyone the same. The decision to incorporate them into your routine depends on your own individual preferences and needs.

For example, don't take a nap if you think it will prevent you from getting your sleep in at night. It's possible that a nap can enhance your overall well-being; however, you never want to take away from your nighttime sleep quality. If you feel you want to try taking naps from time to time, timing your nap strategically is essential. Aim to nap around the midpoint of your day to avoid disrupting your sleep overnight. Fortunately, more employers are providing "nap rooms" for employees to take advantage of during the time, but even if your employer is not one of them, you still might benefit from a snooze on your lunch hour.

Fill Your Time with Things That Matter

You don't have to be an expert to guess the things in life that are most important to people.

Safety, our relationships, our health, and our education are some of the most important aspects of life—to most. However, when really thinking about what it is that means the most to you, think also about how much time you spend away from those things—focused on other things entirely.

It really puts things into perspective when you calculate how little time you really spend focusing on the things most important to you. So, if you want to truly enjoy life, make a plan to spend more time engaging with people and things that matter the most to you.

Start with a little reflection. Remember, when determining what matters to you, there's no right or wrong answer. There's only the truth. Don't waste time denying something that you know matters to you. If going fishing is more important to you than quality family time—so be it. Find time to do more fishing! Obviously, don't neglect your family duties, but take some time for yourself. You'll thank yourself in the long run.

So, take a moment, find a quiet place, clear your mind, and ask yourself—what matters the most?

Properly Manage Your Emotions

Emotions are an integral part of our daily lives; they're there in all of our experiences and all of our reactions. From frustration in traffic to sadness when someone passes and even anger when feeling betrayed, these feelings are all too familiar. However, for some, emotions can take on a more intense and unpredictable form, as well, which in turn can lead to significant highs and lows.

If you find yourself grappling with intense emotions, you may find yourself also oscillating between states of calmness and sudden bursts of sadness or anger. These fluctuations can profoundly impact your relationships and overall well-being, as impulsive actions and regrettable words often follow suit, leading loved ones to learn to stop trusting you, be afraid of your unpredictability, or be constantly worried about upsetting you to the point they're no longer honest with you.

Various factors can contribute to this kind of emotional turbulence, including some genetic predispositions, high or low blood sugar, as well as past traumatic experiences. However, there are some people who have just never learned proper emotional regulation practices. It is a skill like most other things, and it must be modeled and taught. If you find yourself struggling with this, seek guidance from a professional who may be able to help.

It would be beneficial to hone this skill, as it can allow you to gain better control over your overall internal state and lead to greater stability and harmony in your—and your loved ones—life.

Key Takeaways

"In Chapter 4: Keep Yourself Healthy," we learn that there are a myriad of different ways our bodies and minds demand attention. Whether it's finding new activities to explore either by yourself or with your loved ones, you can create deeper connections that last forever and aid in your own mental health by doing things you truly enjoy. Whether it's cooking, hiking, painting, or volunteering, exploring new activities together strengthens bonds and adds excitement to relationships.

In addition to doing things you enjoy, you must also do things that you're maybe not as excited about in order to maintain your overall health. This includes:

- **Prioritizing regular checkups:** Visiting your family physician regularly is essential for maintaining optimal physical health. Regular checkups not only help identify and address health concerns early but also contribute to lower health care costs in the long run. Investing time in preventive care today can save you both time and money down the road.

- **Nourishing your body with what it needs:** Good nutrition and hydration are fundamental for overall health at any age, but this is especially true as we age. A balanced diet rich in essential nutrients supports energy levels, weight management, and disease prevention. Pay attention to signs of inadequate nutrition and prioritize foods that nourish and sustain your body.

- **Practicing good hygiene:** Maintaining proper hygiene is important to both physical and mental health. Brushing your teeth and prioritizing bodily hygiene habits can improve mood, relationships, and cognitive function.

- **Going to the dentist and optometrist:** Recognize the interconnectedness of dental and eye health with mental and physical health and prioritize regular dental checkups to prevent oral health issues that can impact overall well-being. Additionally, ensure regular eye exams to maintain optimal vision and address any potential concerns early.

- **Limiting Screen Time:** Excessive screen time, particularly on social media, can have detrimental effects on both physical and mental health. By setting boundaries and reducing screen time, you can improve sleep quality, reduce eye strain, and enhance your emotional health.

Additional ways to improve your health include:

- **Embracing naps (if it makes sense):** Incorporating short naps into your day can help reduce stress, improve memory, and enhance overall productivity. However, ensure that napping aligns with your sleep patterns and doesn't interfere with nighttime rest.

- **Focusing on what matters to you:** Identify and prioritize the aspects of life that matter most to you. Whether it's spending time with loved ones, pursuing personal goals, or engaging in activities that bring you joy and fulfillment, make sure that you're allocating your time and energy to what truly matters to you specifically.

- **Managing your emotions:** Cultivate emotional resilience by learning strategies to regulate your emotions effectively. Realize that emotional regulation is a skill that needs to be learned and developed. Whether through mindfulness practices, therapy, or self-reflection, developing emotional intelligence can improve relationships and your decision-making skills.

Chapter 5

Live in the Moment

In a world often characterized by hectic schedules, endless to-do lists, and constant distractions, the concept of living in the moment can seem like an unachievable ideal. However, that couldn't be further from the truth. While it may take a little more effort and practice, there are ways to fully engage with the present moment.

In this chapter, we will explore the importance of embracing mindfulness and presence in our daily lives and how doing so can lead to greater happiness, fulfillment, and overall satisfaction with our lives.

We will also learn that living in the moment is about more than just being physically present—it's about fully immersing ourselves in the richness of each experience, whether big or small. It's about savoring the taste of a delicious meal, feeling the warmth of the sun on our skin, or appreciating the beauty of a fleeting sunset. We aren't only physically present but mentally and spiritually living and breathing in every moment.

Buy Yourself Things That Make You Happy

In a world that often emphasizes the importance of selflessness and sacrifice, it's easy to overlook the importance of prioritizing our own needs and desires. However, we have discussed several times in this guide the importance of putting yourself first sometimes, and indulging in occasional treats and purchases for ourselves isn't just a frivolous venture—it's an essential aspect of self-care and your mental well-being. So go out there and buy that coffee you like, get that pair of shoes—we only live once! Just make sure you do it responsibly. Set a budget, stick to the budget, and all will be right in the world! If you prioritize yourself and buying yourself that "thing" that brings you joy, you will find that you'll start looking forward to things just a little bit more.

So next time, you sit down with your budget, add a little allowance for yourself. Buying things that make you happy doesn't have to be a splurge or expensive in the least. It can be as simple or as small as getting a coffee or a candy bar, which are good for any budget!

Make Time to Laugh!

Laughter holds remarkable power as a form of medicine. Have you ever been sad and then watched a funny TV show or movie or maybe even your friend told a joke, and you instantly felt a little better? Well, that's because laughter holds many medicinal benefits. It's just good for the soul. Studies have shown that laughter has a laundry list of benefits, including the fact that it strengthens the immune system, elevates mood, alleviates pain, and shields against the harmful effects of stress.

It's truly just a natural remedy that swiftly restores balance to the mind and body, offering relief from burdens, instilling a little bit of hope, and it can also help foster connections with others. In fact, by embracing laughter in your life—and in the life you share with your loved ones—you boost not only your mood but also your friend's mood and your relationship with one another.

Research even suggests that a strong sense of humor and frequent laughter may contribute to a longer lifespan, particularly among individuals facing serious illnesses such as cancer. Overall, the physical, mental, and social benefits of laughter highlight its invaluable role in promoting health, happiness, and longevity.

Inside Jokes with Loved Ones

If you and your loved ones could live as long as humanly possible by just telling jokes to one another, wouldn't you jump right on board? Well, inside jokes are a great secret language of laughter, a special little code that only you and your loved one can understand. It almost feels like the two of you (or more if there's more than one loved one in on the joke) have created a new language that no one else has ever heard of. While they're generally a little childish, they typically hold a unique power to strengthen bonds by evoking laughter and creating a sense of camaraderie that's exclusive to your relationship. In fact, inside jokes can benefit your relationship by creating:

- **Shared understanding:** Inside jokes create a sense of belonging and even a bit of intimacy. They stem from shared experiences and references that are unique to your friendship and your friendship alone.

- **Instant connection when it's brought up:** Just a word or a phrase referencing this joke can spark laughter and bring back fond memories basically instantly, and connect you and your loved one all over again—no matter how much time has passed since the original joke was formed.

- **Love and appreciation for one another:** This kind of joke also serves as a way to express affection and appreciation without all the mushy gushy talk. If you're the type that shies away from talking about your feelings, this may be a great, intimate bonding experience with your loved one since the joke can signify a depth of connection that goes beyond something surface-level.

When you use fun and laughter as the glue to your relationship, you realize just how powerful joy can be. Laughter is a powerful bonding agent because it reinforces the incredible positivity in your relationship. Jokes and inside jokes contribute to past memories and shared experiences between just the two of you and usually derive from a place of hilarity. However, as they become forged as a bonding tool, they soon become heartwarming, also because they create a true emotional connection.

Friends who have inside jokes can instantly have their spirits lifted during tough times, and sometimes laughter is the best medicine for negativity or sadness. Other benefits of inside jokes in laughing together are the fact that they:

- **Cultivate shared experiences:** Anything can become

an inside joke. However, they are generally derived after something happened during an activity or adventure together. The joke plays node to the fact that you experienced something special together, but it's important to note that you should continue to have shared experiences together in the future. You never know how many inside jokes you could develop as time goes on.

- **Are playful with one another:** Allowing inside jokes to naturally emerge from funny situations or conversations is a great way to be playful with one another and to simply have fun. Embrace spontaneity and humor in all of your interactions, and make sure that you continue to spread light and joy to your loved one. They may need it more than you realize.

- **Encourage exclusivity:** While it's generally more agreeable to be "inclusive" rather than "exclusive," if you're looking at growing the bond in one specific relationship, that call can be completely up to you. You can share inside jokes openly, and you can certainly welcome others into the fold. Think of it as a special and secret club. If you want to explain the joke, you can, but if you don't want to, you don't have to. You and your loved ones have the right to make that call. It can be something just for you, if you would prefer it remain an "inside" joke and be more private in nature.

- **Are personal:** Inside jokes are like secret treasures, personalized to your relationship, and they showcase the uniqueness of your bond together. Even if you did share it with others, it may be possible it was a "had to be there" situation or that others might not get your humor directly. That is perfectly okay. Just enjoy the joke with your loved one.

- **Strengthen trust:** Referencing an inside joke signifies trust and closeness because it reiterates the fact that the two of you have something special in the first place. It also showed that at some point in your relationship, you had both created an environment where you both felt comfortable and understood. That is an invaluable experience to have in a relationship.

- **Are timeless:** Inside jokes have a timeless quality. They can resurface after years and still evoke the same laughter and warmth as they did the very first time they were said.

Splurge on Things Occasionally

This can go along with buying yourself things that make you happy—but it does go well beyond that, too. Some cultures glorify frugality and restraint, and, therefore, the very idea of splurging may seem frivolous and unmerited. However, there are times when that splurge means more than anything else!

While it's true, money cannot buy happiness, there are times when a splurge can bring us joy. Maybe it's that big trip you've always wanted to go on or that designer bag you've never been able to afford. Whatever it is—if it truly could bring you joy and it's worth planning for—do it!

Times when splurging makes sense include when you are:

- **Celebrating achievements and milestones:** Splurging is a powerful way to acknowledge and celebrate your accomplishments, big and small. Whether you've reached a career milestone, achieved a personal goal, or overcome some sort of significant challenge, treating yourself to something special that you wouldn't normally give to yourself is a meaningful way to honor your achievements and reward yourself for your hard work and dedication. By rewarding yourself, you're also opening up more opportunities and incentives to reach other milestones; so in essence, the splurge can truly incentivize you to do your best and reach for the stars.

- **Creating lasting memories:** If a splurge can create a memory that lasts a lifetime, it's worth it! In a year, two years, ten years, we won't worry about the money that was spent—but we can remember a once-in-a-lifetime opportunity.

As with everything, splurging should only be done occasionally. Some practical tips include:

- **Setting a budget:** Determine how much you can comfortably afford to spend on splurges each month, and stick to it. Setting a budget helps ensure that you're being financially responsible while still allowing yourself the freedom to indulge from time to time.

- **Choosing experiences over possessions:** As stated before, if a splurge can be in the form of a once-in-a-lifetime experience, it's worth it! Although that designer purse may be nice to have, if you have to choose between it and a once-in-a-lifetime opportunity, it may be worth prioritizing the experience over the material possession.

- **Practice gratitude:** Take a moment to appreciate and savor the indulgences and extravagances you allow yourself. If you're not the type to splurge often, allow yourself time to enjoy it when you do.

Express Yourself Artistically

Do you love getting lost in a painting, humming along to your favorite song, or jotting down your thoughts in a journal? Well, here's some great news—not only is it enjoyable, but it's actually good for your brain and your relationships to focus on these artistic ventures! Expressing yourself creatively can help you feel more connected to yourself as well as those around you. This can lead to improved mental health and a huge boost in self-esteem.

Human beings have a wonderful ability to think outside the box and come up with unique ideas, which is how art is even in existence. To be able to creatively express yourself is a true gift and has several benefits, such as stress relief and the ability to be placed in a "flow state," which means you become hyper-focused on a task or activity (also known as "in the zone"), leading to feelings of euphoria and accomplishment.

Benefits of Painting, Writing, and Listening to Music

At one point or another in your life, you have likely experienced loneliness. It's not at all a pleasant experience. After all, human beings are social creatures by nature. But did you know that artistic expression can help you build a stronger sense of character and work through complicated emotions? Did you also know that by tapping into your artistic side, you can express feelings and emotions that are sometimes too difficult to fabricate into words?

Studies show that when you're able to let your creativity flow, you not only reduce anxiety and stress but can also provide much-needed nourishment to your brain. In fact, you don't even have to be an artist to benefit from art. Simply immersing yourself in it can have many positive benefits to your brain, such as increased blood flow, which can induce a "pleasure response."

But it isn't just painting that works well for our bodies. Expressive writing has been shown to enhance our health and happiness in many ways, too. For example, studies have shown that writing can be beneficial in controlling and reducing the severity of pain, as well as alleviating depression.

Like painting and writing, music is another powerful artistic tool. In fact, listening to music releases oxytocin in the brain, a hormone that plays a key role in promoting positive social bonds and helping us feel calmer and more relaxed.

Create a Bucket List

Have you ever thought about all the things that you would like to accomplish in your lifetime? Have you ever made a list? Most people have a pretty long list, and it's only natural to wonder if you will ever get the opportunity to achieve them.

Whether they seem like far-fetched travel destinations, major career benchmarks, or even just personal growth ideologies, some of them may seem out of grasp. However, a bucket list is still an incredible way to compile all of the ideas you have for your life in one thoughtful list.

A bucket list, simply put, is a list of all the things you'd like to do before you "kick the bucket." Bucket lists have the power to help guide you in your journey, inform your decisions, and add true purpose to your everyday life. By merely existing, your bucket list can singlehandedly put you on a trajectory that is essential to creating the life you want.

Let's face it, life is short! Creating a bucket list can help you think of what is truly important to you and how you would like to live your life from this point forward! With the list's help, you can take these super big, almost unobtainable feats and break them down in a way that is completely attainable.

So, what should you put on your bucket list?

Well, the answer to that is completely up to you! However, based on studies, there are usually hugely common themes. These themes include the desire to travel, the desire to accomplish a personal goal, spending quality time with friends and family, financial stability, and the desire to do a dangerous or daring activity.

How to Get Started Writing a List

Step One: Self-Reflect and Brainstorm

At this stage, you might find yourself falling into one of two categories: either you're bursting with ideas and dreams, eager to jot them all down, or you're feeling a bit lost and have no idea where to even start.

Wherever category you find yourself in, start off by establishing a dedicated space to organize your thoughts. Consider options like a journal for your bucket list or even a simple Word document you can update as needed—the choice is yours and yours alone.

Next, dive into a fruitful brainstorming session. What immediately comes to mind? What have you always wanted to do but never found the time for? What aspirations are on hold due to financial constraints? At this brainstorming stage, remember that no idea is too grand or too small—capture everything on paper. You can always weed down later!

While it is true that some people may want to include fantastical dreams that might never come to fruition, others may truly prefer to focus on tangible, achievable goals. For instance, going to the moon may be a wonderful ambition, but it may not be feasible in reality. While such aspirations are undeniably fun, the most rewarding goals tend to be grounded in everyday reality so that you can actually reach them. While you're writing, it may be a good idea to jot down a few notes next to each "idea" to differentiate between short-term objectives and long-term ambitions.

Remember, everyone's list is unique, shaped by factors like age, cultural background, and even personal experiences. Some people may put something on a bucket list that you have already done—or do frequently, so make sure that the list is yours and yours alone. Embrace this diversity and keep dreaming big as you move forward.

Step 2: Organize Your Ideas

Research from Sanford suggests that most bucket list goals fall into six main categories, though you're not limited to these. They simply serve as a starting point to stimulate your imagination.

These categories include:

- Desire to travel (e.g., going to the Mayan ruins or exploring Egyptian pyramids)

- Personal goals (e.g., writing a book or becoming your own boss)

- Achieving life milestones (e.g., having children)

- Spending quality time with loved ones

- Financial well-being (e.g., earning one million dollars)

- Daring activities (e.g., swimming with sharks or jumping out of a plane)

With these categories in mind, you likely have a slew of new ideas for your bucket list.

Step 3: Trim It Down and Set Timeframes

These time frames are not set in stone, but by trimming down your ideas to those that take precedence, you can hopefully set achievable goals to actually cross some things off your list. You can start by setting an age "Ten Things to Do in Ten Years" or something of that nature. Give yourself plenty of time, especially for the items on the list that may take a lot of planning or saving.

Step 4: Start Updating and Crossing Things Off

With your list in hand, it's time to embark on your bucket list journey and start ticking off those experiences! Aim to accomplish at least one item every year or two to maintain momentum and keep yourself motivated.

Remember:

Bucket lists may be twenty items deep, or there could be hundreds of items on your list. There's no one-size-fits-all answer to what your list should be comprised of, as everyone's bucket list is unique to them and their experiences. It's advisable to strike a balance between short-term and long-term goals. That way, you can feel like you're accomplishing things you've always wanted to do—in a short span of time while also holding onto big dreams for the larger items. There is also no order in which to cross things off your list. Aim for a list that allows you to regularly check off accomplishments as often as you feel you need to in order to maintain your motivation.

Key Takeaways

In "Chapter 5: Live in the Moment," we discuss life as a journey. It's important to prioritize treating yourself occasionally as a form of self-care and mental well-being. Splurge on yourself, especially when it is in celebration of your achievements or to create lasting memories, but do so responsibly. Indulging in activities that bring you joy, laughter, and relaxation is essential for overall happiness and health. In fact, those are some of the biggest medicines you can experience in your life. Laughter especially, which is a byproduct of joy and happiness. Incorporate laughter into your life as it offers numerous physical, mental, and social benefits. Remember that it not only allows you to grow closer to others, but it also relaxes the body, boosts the immune system, and relieves stress for you and all involved.

And finally, remember to express yourself creatively through painting, listening to music, and writing to give yourself a mental boost and aid in brain functionality. And while you're at it, create a bucket list comprised of goals and aspirations to add purpose and motivation to your life. Bucket lists encourage self-reflection, inspire personal growth, and provide opportunities for adventure and fulfillment.

In summary, prioritize your happiness through occasional indulgence, laughter, creative expression, and goal-setting. These practices contribute to overall well-being, resilience, and a deeper sense of fulfillment in your journey to love your life.

Chapter 6

Socialize and Experience Joy

In a fast-paced world where we're often consumed by daily tasks and responsibilities, it's easy to overlook the importance of social connections. But as we've heard in this guide a time or two—human beings are social creatures, and that means that socialization is a major cornerstone in remaining happy and healthy and therefore critical in your journey to love your life.

Identify Your Role Models

Think back to when you were a young child. Who did you want to be when you grew up? Was it your favorite superhero? Was it a movie star or another celebrity? What about your dad, mom, aunt or uncle?

At some point in all of our lives, we find people to look up to—and even as adults, we still have our heroes or people who have a profound influence over us in one facet or another. These people are called role models. And put simply, a role model is someone who serves as an example and someone who encompasses something that others look up to and is considered worthy of imitation on some level.

People have role models at all stages of their lives, but role models are usually most impressionable on children and younger adults. But as we grow older, these role models begin to shift away from superheroes and celebrities and get a little closer to home. They become colleagues, parents, grandparents, neighbors, teachers, etc.

Why Are Role Models Important?

Even though we all look up to someone at one point or another, we rarely give the question of why they're important much thought. However, the truth of the matter is that we all need role models to some degree. They teach us important life lessons, and their actions generally have a profound influence over us and our lives as we know them.

Positive role models influence our actions, often in the form of imitation (kind of a "monkey see, monkey do" idea), and motivate us to be just as great as they are! In fact, studies show that children, as the impressionable youth that they are, learn better when they watch appropriate behavior or action. That is why parents are oftentimes told to model the behavior they wish to see in their children. If the proper role model is found, children have a greater success rate in achieving goals that they have set for themselves.

What Does a Good Role Model Do?

The effects of a positive role model cannot be overstated, even outside of childhood. Oftentimes, when you're going for that promotion at work, it's recommended that you first shadow someone else—someone a little more senior, someone who can become a role model to you. Their primary job is to inspire and motivate while modeling positive behaviors.

Role models have the platform to inspire, which is why it's important for role models to try and be a good example.

Children, teenagers, and adults all face challenges. Challenges are part of life, and the truth of the matter is choosing a role model who can show their humanity, face their own challenges, and bounce back even in the face of adversity is inspiring! Finding appropriate role models, even in your adulthood, to help guide you through life is absolutely a phenomenal, inspiring, and encouraging feat. The best way to find the right one for you is to ask yourself what you hope to achieve—and what you would like to learn from a role model. Looking at what you hope to gain from mimicking someone else can help determine the best role model for you, but regardless of who you choose or what you choose to learn from them, go through your life and find the best role models you can!

Quiet the Inner Critic

It is unrealistic to expect to silence your inner critic completely. In fact, you wouldn't want to do it completely. Your inner critic can be harnessed and aid you in becoming the best version of yourself that you can be by allowing you the opportunity to consistently grow and develop your skills and behavior. There is nothing wrong with improving yourself. And that little voice inside your head can help.

However, if your inner critic is constantly spewing negativity about all of your actions or is a little too hard on you, then it may be necessary to battle the critic inside of you. According to leading psychologists, the best way to do this is to imagine—every time your inner critic speaks—that a friend or family member answers it.

This can truly help reframe negativity and allow you to see yourself in a more positive light, even when improvements really do need to be made.

Go out and Meet New People

As we have discussed throughout this guide, relationships, in general, can have a major impact on your health. However, it isn't always easy to develop or maintain friendships. As we get older, our time is cut drastically short due to obligations and responsibilities. The friends you have as an adult, are typically friends you have had for a long time—but they don't have to be your only friends forever. By understanding the importance of social connection in your life and what you can do to help build and even nurture the friendships and relationships you already have, as well as the new ones you gain, you will be able to truly solidify deep and meaningful connections for your lifetime.

After all, good friends are good for your health, and the truth of the matter is quality is definitely more important than quantity. But there is nothing wrong with getting out there to meet new friends from time to time. Friends can help you celebrate good times and provide support during the more challenging times. Friends prevent isolation and loneliness and offer companionship when you need it the most. Finding good, quality friends can:

- Increase your sense of belonging and purpose (which we discussed being a huge benefit to loved ones)

- Boost your happiness and reduce your stress

- Improve your self-esteem and self-worth

- Help you cope with traumas, such as divorce, illness, job loss, or even the death of another loved one

- Encourage you to change or avoid unhealthy lifestyle habits, such as excessive drinking, lack of exercise, or smoking

- Reduce your risk of depression, high blood pressure, or an unhealthy body mass index

- Help you live longer

So, how do you meet new people and make new friends? The same way that you nurture the friendships you already have! It doesn't take an advanced degree. Set aside time, go out for drinks with coworkers, reconnect with people you've lost touch with, introduce yourself to neighbors, start a book club, go to a poetry slam—whatever your interests are, consider meeting people through that outlet!

Don't forget that there are likely people you have thought about reaching out to that you never did; try and recall anyone who stands out in your memory as someone you'd like to know better. Reach out. Extend an invite to coffee. Moreover, don't limit yourself to one strategy for meeting people. And be persistent. For example, try several of these ideas to engage with others:

- **Attend community events:** As we discussed, search for groups or clubs that revolve around an interest or hobby you have. You can likely find these groups online or in a newspaper.

- **Volunteer:** Offer your time or talents at a hospital, place of worship, museum, community center, charitable group, or other organization. You can form strong connections when you work with people who have mutual interests. Besides, if someone is volunteering their time, it may be safe to assume that they have a bit of compassion as well—which is a great friendship quality.

- **Join a faith community:** Take advantage of special activities and get-to-know-you events or gatherings at your church. These can sometimes be some of the richest forms of friendships if you have a particular interest in religion.

Go On Dates—With Yourself and Others

To help you better navigate the world of dating, you can begin your journey by first dating yourself. It's difficult to evaluate the suitability of someone else as a partner if you haven't even taken the time to get to know yourself first. If you don't know who you are, how will you know what you want in another person? Your relationship with others will be affected by how you may view yourself—so it truly is important to get to know yourself.If you've had a hard time dating, either because you've been rejected, you're constantly disappointed, or you're just not meeting the right type of partner, it might be time to go inward and really search yourself, your likes, dislikes, and your preferences.

Even if you're not really looking for a romantic relationship at this time, it can still be encouraging and beneficial to spend a little time with yourself. By spending time thinking about your likes and dislikes as well as your goals, you can truly learn a lot about yourself.

You'll become more comfortable just being you and participating in activities with others—even if it isn't in a romantic sense.

Steps to Take before Dating Yourself

When you meet someone online or through an app, you can get to know one another through messages before you ever meet in person. You make conversation, ask questions, and build a rapport. Then, when you meet in person, you usually eat, drink, or participate in some type of activity that you've already established the two of you may be interested in. The entire point of this is the fact that you're assessing and learning about one another to determine whether you want to take the relationship further.

When you date yourself, you need to do the exact same thing—except you don't really have a choice. You have to take the relationship further. You're stuck with yourself. But you're able to determine your likes, dislikes, passions, vulnerabilities, and values. You can learn what makes you tick, you can learn what means the most to you—and you can find out what about yourself that you may not like in a partner and determine if that's something you should fix about yourself or potentially have more grace about when it comes to others.

Ultimately, getting to know yourself in this way really opens your eyes to a world of possibilities—not only for you to capture a more fulfilling romance later on, but also what others may see in you and opportunities to grow.

Self-Care

This guide is all about fifty ways to love your life. The key word is "your." This is your life. This is your health. This is your well-being. A common theme is all about self-care. By going on an exploration of who you are as a person, it is important to remember to take care of yourself. This could mean one of the dates you go on with yourself is to a spa—or it could mean getting ready for a date with yourself as you would a romantic partner.

Take a nice, long bubble bath with candles. Dress in your best. Put on the expensive makeup you save for special occasions or that really luxurious cologne. Go get a mani/pedi; go get that massage. Do something that promotes you, your health, and your happiness—in all your glory!

Be Kind to Yourself

If your negative inner voice is chiming in, remind it to be kind. Negative self-talk can be just as toxic as an abusive partner. Treat yourself with compassion. Think about your favorite person in the world. Would you tell that person they looked bad in that outfit? Would you call them names or belittle them?

The answer should be a resounding "no"!

So when that inner critic chastises you for making mistakes or decreases your sense of self-worth and motivation, remind yourself that you're also only human—just like your favorite person. Give yourself some grace. And love yourself just as much as you love that person you thought of!

Get Rid of Distractions

Distractions are oftentimes killers of self-care. Not the typical distractions such as your phone or social media. These distractions are even worse—because they're the ones that distract you from providing yourself with the care necessary to flourish.

Or, even worse—they take the place of self-care.

If your self-care activities include any type of desensitizing by binging food, alcohol, drugs, or digital media in an effort to numb yourself, you are allowing self-care distractions to take control of your life. It is possible to feel "joy" or "happiness" in doing these things in the short term—but only in the short term, as they are killers of the overarching idea of self-care. That isn't to say that you can't enjoy food, digital media, or alcohol—but misusing them to a degree of preventing yourself from the self-care you desperately need to flourish is not healthy. If you find yourself doing this regularly, you may want to seek professional guidance, but some steps to start include:

- **Journal writing:** Getting to the root of your feelings is sometimes the best way to battle issues.

- **Practicing deep breathing and meditation:** This is a self-care routine that is quick and efficient and works great against self-care distraction because you are immediately replacing it with something true to self-care.

Self-Love

When dating yourself, self-care is the ultimate necessity. By being kind and compassionate to yourself, getting rid of distractions that can prevent you from making time for self-care, and learning to truly love yourself, you are able to care for yourself in an appropriate and healthy way—a way that can create the best version of yourself, for not only your own mental health but also for others so that they may enjoy you at your optimal level.

You have likely heard that when you're on an airplane, it is imperative that you put your own oxygen mask on before helping others. This is the same thing. It is important to focus and love yourself before you can properly love anyone. That isn't to say that loving someone, even in your flawed state, and them loving you back can't help you learn to appreciate yourself through their perspective. But it is to say that it is better to love yourself through your own lens eventually, too. This is only accomplished by getting to know yourself completely and fully. And again—this is best accomplished by dating yourself.

Confidence is beautiful, and you deserve to have that confidence. Understand that your ideas and thoughts have value, know that for others to respect you, you must first respect yourself, and realize that even if you don't always agree with what you have done, give yourself a little grace and maintain a positive image of yourself—just as you would a loved one.

Do Something for Someone in Need

Another way to socialize and experience joy is by experiencing the joy that comes from helping those in need. Performing acts of kindness for those in need not only benefits the recipient but can also bring immense satisfaction and fulfillment to the giver. Whether it's volunteering at a local shelter, donating to a charity you find appealing, or simply offering a helping hand to someone in distress or in need of a skill that you can provide to them, these gestures have the power to make a meaningful difference in the lives of others. Who knows? It may even cause a ripple effect and breathe a little more positivity in the world in general. Ways to help people in need include:

- **Volunteering your time:** One of the most impactful ways to help those in need is by volunteering your time and skills. Whether it's serving meals at a local soup kitchen or homeless shelter, tutoring underprivileged children, or participating in community cleanups, volunteering your time allows you to directly engage with and support those facing challenges in your community.

- **Donate to charities:** There are so many charities you can choose from. Financial contributions to reputable organizations can provide essential resources and support to those in need. Whether it's donating to organizations that provide food and shelter to animals or the homeless, support medical research, or aid disaster relief, every contribution—no matter how small—can make a huge impact.

- **Random acts of kindness:** Sometimes, the simplest acts of kindness can have the greatest impact on someone's day. Whether it's offering a listening ear to a friend in need, helping an elderly neighbor with household chores, buying a meal for a homeless person, bringing flowers to hospice care, or providing a skill to someone who may not be able to afford it—these small gestures of compassion and empathy can brighten someone's day and remind them that they are not alone.

- **Spreading awareness:** Although direct acts of service and giving are amazing, sometimes, raising awareness about issues or charities and advocating for change can make an even bigger difference. Whether it's sharing information on social media, participating in fundraising events, or engaging in community activism, spreading awareness can help mobilize support and resources to address pressing social issues and create positive change.

- **Leading by example:** Just as you need a role model, sometimes the biggest opportunity for helping someone is by being *their* role model. By embodying kindness and compassion in your own actions and interactions, you can inspire others to do the same. Whether it's through modeling what true empathy and generosity look like in your daily life or actively encouraging others to join you in acts of service and giving, leading by example can create a culture that benefits everyone.

Performing acts of kindness for those in need is a powerful way to make a positive impact in the world and give you a great bit of positive social interaction in the meantime. Whether through volunteering, donating, offering acts of kindness, spreading awareness, or leading by example, each of us has the power to contribute to creating a more compassionate and caring society.

Key Takeaways

In "Chapter 6: Socialize and Experience Joy," we discuss the importance of social connections. As we've heard in this guide, human beings are social creatures, and that means that socialization is a major cornerstone in remaining happy and healthy and therefore critical in your journey to Love Your Life. The first step in socializing and experiencing joy is with our loved ones, of course, whether that be with friends, family, or a romantic partner. Investing in relationships offers numerous benefits, from increased happiness to reduced stress and improved health. Make sure that you prioritize quality over quantity and actively seek opportunities to make new, quality friends and nurture the relationships you currently have.

Beyond your loved ones, there is another important relationship to establish—and Chapter 6 discusses that at length—and that is a role model. By identifying positive role models, you can gain inspiration and motivation and be guided toward the overarching goal of betterment as you shape your behavior to mimic theirs.

While finding an appropriate role model in life is essential to grow and develop and gain inspiration, it is important to know that you, as you are now, are worthy of love and admiration. Quieting the inner critic and nurturing self-compassion is also an essential aspect of mental well-being. By reframing negative self-talk and practicing self-care, we can develop a more supportive inner voice and build resilience against self-doubt. Dating yourself is also a great way to reframe your negativity. Pretend like you're talking to a loved one rather than yourself in order to quiet negativity when it comes to yourself. Engage in self-care practices to cultivate a love for yourself to deepen your own understanding of your own identity.

Once you have cultivated love for yourself, you can begin to love others more fully and appropriately, including loving them to a degree in which you crave the act of spreading kindness and compassion through acts of service.

Chapter 7

Celebrate

Celebrating your life goes beyond just cheering for yourself. It is all about really cherishing your life, your loved ones, and everything your life encompasses. Your experiences and loved ones truly bring uniqueness to the table that is worth being celebrated day in and day out. Celebrating your life is critical in truly showing them how much you love being alive, and even if you're having a bad day, bad month, bad year—take time to celebrate the good in your life!

Approach Every Day Like It Could Be the Best Day of Your Life

Every single waking day should be spent like it is your last here on earth. While that isn't exactly feasible, it is a great exercise if you're looking for more ways to love your life and show gratitude for it. Let's face it—life is full of surprises. You never know for certain what any given day is going to look like, and likewise, you never know exactly where you might end up or what you might accomplish in the future—no matter how much you plan.

Sometimes, life bites us in the rear—but it's important to remember that life is also full of happiness.

Throw out the fear of what anyone might think of you, and live with intention and purpose. If tomorrow really was your last day, think about how you would live. This is a repeat exercise that can do wonders for your mental clarity.

What would you say to a loved one? What activity would you choose to do? These questions are critical because the reality is that even though today may not be your last day, our days are still numbered. Every second of every day matters, and time as we know it is incredibly valuable because of this fact.

So, do this exercise—ask yourself the questions, and live your life like it's your last as often as you can. Write that book you've always told yourself you would write, paint that masterpiece, gather up the courage to do that thing you've been putting off for all those years. Go tell your loved ones you love them.

Approach every day like this, and you'll be glad when the time comes that you didn't waste a moment—and you'll learn to love your life all the more during the journey.

Start a Gratitude Journal

We have discussed a gratitude journal previously in this guide, but only briefly. A gratitude journal can be an excellent way to celebrate your life because gratitude plays an important role in our psychological well-being and self-actualization.

Learning to express gratitude can lead to increased feelings of happiness, satisfaction, meaningfulness, and studies also show a higher rate of productivity. When you sit down to write in your journal, consider what you'll write about. It is suggested to think about all aspects of your life:

- Your friends and family
- Living beings and inanimate objects
- Experiences or opportunities
- Events

Other forms of the "gratitude journal" include the gratitude jar and the gratitude letter. Each of these can be a great tool to reflect on the positive aspects of life.

- **Gratitude Jar:** This is a fun exercise that is especially useful for children or as a romantic gift between partners. Individuals are encouraged to write on pieces of paper and put their gratitude notes in the jar. On special days, you write, and on other days, you pull a note as a reminder of things you should feel grateful for.

- **Gratitude Letter:** Sometimes, it's easier to express your thoughts and feelings in a letter rather than saying them in person or giving them to someone else to read, and maybe you're not interested in creating an entire journal. Yearly gratitude letters can suffice and be a great reflective tool.

Appreciate the Journey

Life as we know it is a journey, an ever-unfolding story filled with twists, turns, challenges, and triumphs. While it can be easy to fixate on reaching destinations or achieving goals, true fulfillment lies in embracing the journey itself.

Find Beauty in the Ordinary

Life's greatest joys often lie in the simplest of moments. By attuning our senses to the beauty that surrounds us, we can find wonder and delight in every day and even the mundane. Whether it's the laughter of loved ones, the warmth of the sun hitting our skin, or the melody of birds chirping outside our windowsills, beauty surrounds us each and every day.

Embrace the Uncertainty

The journey of life is inherently uncertain, filled with unknowns and unexpected challenges. Rather than fearing uncertainty, we can learn to embrace it as an essential part of growth and discovery. By cultivating resilience and adaptability, we can navigate life's twists and turns with grace and courage and learn to trust in our ability to overcome obstacles and emerge stronger than we were before.

Learn from Challenges: Life's journey is not without its challenges, but just like facing uncertainty, facing life's challenges and adversity, we grow and evolve. Rather than viewing challenges as obstacles to be avoided, we can see them as opportunities for learning and transformation. By embracing setbacks with resilience and determination, we emerge stronger, wiser, and more compassionate individuals.

Celebrate Progress, Not Perfection: In a world obsessed with success and achievement, it's easy to overlook the value of progress made along the way. Instead of fixating on perfection, we can celebrate small victories and milestones, recognizing that growth is a gradual and ongoing process. By embracing our journey with patience and self-compassion, we honor the unique path that has led us to where we are today.

Ultimately, life's journey is a precious gift, meant to be savored and cherished with each step we take up life's mountainside.

Celebrate Special Days

Celebrating is good for people. It's an opportunity for activity, conversation, laughter, and excitement. Parties can mean games and singing and even dancing. But more than anything—it means joy. Celebrating special days is abundantly important on this journey of loving your life.

Although there are more "special days" than holidays, holidays are generally the first that come to mind when discussing a unique blend of festivities, joy, and togetherness. Invite your family and friends to celebrate as much as humanly possible. Whether you're someone extroverted, reveling in lively gatherings with friends and family, or someone who prefers to relish the tranquility of a little more intimate celebrations, there's a special place for loved ones among it all. Make sure that you acknowledge those birthdays, those anniversaries, and the holidays—and enjoy them with people you love!

Make Traditions Together

While you're celebrating important days, make sure that you take the time to make traditions! That way, the celebration gets to happen on a repeating basis and gives you something to look forward to!

Family traditions are etched into us from the moment we're born. They are usually more prominent around the holiday season, encompassing activities like Christmas caroling, baking cookies, decorating, and indulging in Christmas movie marathons. Each family has its unique way of celebrating and its very own list of traditions. Some people have a strong foundation in their traditions. Some of the traditions that you personally have might have derived from your family, and others you may have just developed on your own. Whatever the case, traditions truly help us cultivate a connection with others. It is because it enables us the opportunity to have meaningful shared experiences together and enriches our lives because we have things we can look forward to. Whether it's your family member or your best friend, you can establish some sort of tradition. In fact, it may be possible that you're closer to your friends than you are to your own family. That's when traditions with them may be even more important, but why not have a game night, an annual Friendsgiving, a Christmas Eve cocktail party, etc.?

You can completely start from scratch, or you can bring ideas together from your own already-established, traditions. Some fun traditions you can start with include:

- **Choosing a Christmas Tree Together:** If your family ventures into the cold to select the perfect Christmas tree, why not make a special tradition out of it (if it isn't already) and make it fun!

- **Festive Baking:** Would Christmas even be Christmas without cookies? Rather than watching someone you love bake, try making it a family affair (consider even including your kids or pets into the mix!).

- **Holiday Cards:** When sending out holiday cards, keep everyone in mind. Invite family over for a fun day of eggnog and cheer while you get your pictures made!

- **Participating in Christmas Movie Marathons:** In the wintertime, there is honestly nothing better than cozying up on the sofa with a mug full of hot cocoa and binge-watching some of your favorite Christmas movies. Enjoy this with people you love!

- **Playing in the Snow:** If there's snow, go play in it! This is especially great for children, but no matter the age you are (or the other participants), everyone is sure to have a blast! Make it a tradition on the first big snow of the year to go out and have a blast with friends or family! You will love your life a whole heck of a lot more!

Remember, traditions don't just have to be around the holidays, either! You can create a tradition for any time and any place! Just make sure you're surrounded by love!

Get Together with Loved Ones

The importance of family is often overlooked in today's digitally saturated world. Yet, even with the screens and social media platforms, the essence of human connection remains a vital aspect of our mental and physical well-being. Studies on this matter have shown the detrimental effects of excessive social media use on loneliness, and it highlights the indispensable role of face-to-face interactions.

Why is family important?

Spending quality time with family members has been found to garner a multitude of benefits, including increased happiness, reduced stress and anxiety, and a healthier lifestyle. Family serves as a cornerstone for personal development, instilling essential values and fostering mental resilience. Familial bonds are of great significance.

Some more benefits include:

- **Improved mental health:** Engaging in face-to-face interactions with family members significantly reduces the prevalence of depression, anxiety, and other mental health disorders. The emotional support garnered from physical presence serves as a lifeline during challenging times.

- **Children performing better academically:** If you have children, it is important to understand that children who spend quality time with their families tend to excel academically. By fostering open communication and emphasizing the value of education, parents play a pivotal role in nurturing their children's academic success.

- **Lowered risk of behavioral issues:** Again, if you have children, family bonding activities provide a constructive outlet for pent-up emotions, which can reduce the likelihood of behavioral issues such as violence and substance abuse later on.

- **Boosted self-confidence:** Family support cultivates a

sense of belonging and acceptance, which can develop self-esteem and confidence in both children and adults.

- **Learning parental skills:** The dynamics within a family unit serve as a training ground for future caregiving roles. Children observe and emulate parental behaviors.

- **Learning effective conflict resolution:** Navigating conflicts within the family unit fosters essential interpersonal skills, including communication, negotiation, and problem-solving. These skills are invaluable for navigating relationships outside the familial context.

- **Reduced stress:** Strong family bonds provide a support network for coping with stress and adversity. Open communication and shared experiences alleviate stress and promote emotional well-being.

- **Higher adaptability and resilience:** A cohesive family unit instills a sense of security and belonging, empowering individuals to navigate life's challenges with confidence and resilience.

- **Enhanced physical health:** Engaging in physical activities and sharing meals with family members promotes better health outcomes, including improved diet, fitness, and overall well-being.

- **Longer life expectancy:** The cumulative benefits of strong family relationships contribute to increased longevity and a higher quality of life. Research indicates that individuals with robust social networks tend to live longer and healthier lives.

Of course, the reality is that not everyone is fortunate enough to have their biological family. That doesn't mean that you can't still belong or have family! Families can look different from one group to the next. As long as you surround yourself with people you love and who help you feel as though you belong—you're all set! You will learn to love your life with the people that matter!

Learn New Ways to Unwind and Enjoy Life

Relaxation might sound simple, but in reality, it can be quite challenging to achieve. There are numerous factors that can make unwinding difficult. Whether it's feelings of guilt about prioritizing personal time, the relentless pace of your daily life (i.e., you can't stop thinking about all those chores you have to do, or that report that was due three hours ago), or even underlying conditions like anxiety. All the things from our lives that pile up can make finding moments of peace feel like an uphill battle.

While we're on the hunt for relaxation, it's not uncommon to turn to activities that seem soothing but end up leaving us feeling drained, such as indulging in substances or endlessly scrolling through social media feeds. However, there are countless stress-reduction techniques available that offer more sustainable relief.

It's essential to recognize that relaxation is a deeply personal experience, and what works for one person may not work for another. It's okay if certain relaxation strategies don't resonate with you. The key is to explore different approaches and pay attention to how your body responds. Understanding your body's cues can guide you toward the techniques that truly rejuvenate and replenish your energy.

Taking a few minutes to sit quietly and focus on deep breathing can instantly bring a sense of relaxation. You can pair this with a little yoga or meditation, too, or maybe your relaxation works best by strapping on the headphones and listening to music or binge-watching your favorite TV show. Whatever the case, make sure you find what works for you—and just relax.

Find Ways to Make Every Day Special

Embracing simplicity doesn't equate to complacency or to being okay with a dull existence; rather, it opens doors to a more fulfilling and enjoyable life. By simplifying our lifestyles, we are able to gain precious time, space, and energy to engage in more activities that bring us joy and make each day feel special in its own right. Transforming ordinary days into extraordinary experiences is a skill that improves with practice, and it's one that can bring forth a ton of joy and excitement. By adopting a mindset of mindfulness and creativity, we can elevate mundane tasks and routines into sources of happiness and satisfaction. Steps to making every day special include:

- **Celebrating the ordinary:** We don't have to reserve celebrations for big or momentous occasions. By intentionally slowing down and appreciating the beauty in everyday moments, we can cultivate a deeper sense of joy and fulfillment in our lives. Now, that's not to say you have to make a big deal out of every day but think about treating yourself from time to time just because it's Tuesday.

- **Start the day mindfully:** Your mind is your biggest resource and tool. By beginning each day with activities that resonate with us can help set a positive tone for the rest of the day. Whether it's savoring a quiet moment with a cup of coffee or indulging in a favorite hobby, investing a little in ourselves at the start of each day can help create a sense of joy and purposefulness.

- **Add luxury when possible:** Simplifying our possessions can afford us the opportunity to invest in high-quality experiences and items that bring us genuine pleasure. By prioritizing quality over quantity, we can enhance our daily lives with little luxuries that spark joy and elevate our surroundings. Everyone wants to feel pampered, including yourself. Have you ever gotten up, dressed to the nines in a brand-new outfit, thrown on an expensive watch or piece of jewelry, and just gone out to run your errands or grab a cup of coffee? This has been proven to strengthen self-esteem and create a more joyful experience.

- **End each day on a positive note:** Just as we begin our days with intention, we should also conclude them in the same manner. Whether it's unwinding with a favorite book or practicing self-care, ending the day on a positive note sets the stage for restful sleep and rejuvenation.

In essence, making every day feel special is a matter of perspective and conscious choice. By recognizing beauty on a Tuesday and infusing our lives with as many moments of joy and gratitude as we can, we can transform ordinary days into extraordinary experiences.

Consciously Work to Be Positive

As we learned at the beginning of this guide, life is all about making the most out of what you are given (or that you have made for yourself). No matter what's happening in our lives, we can always take time to appreciate what we do have. Positive thinking is critical to not only improving your health—both mentally and physically—but also to improving your life as you know it. It's important to continue to make conscious efforts to apply the techniques in this guide to evoke as much positivity as you humanly can.

The first—and arguably the best—way to consciously work to be more positive is to stop the negative self-talk. This quickly reduces stress and aids in your journey to looking at the world more optimistically.

So, what is negative self-talk?

- **Magnifying/embellishing:** You magnify the negative aspects of a situation and filter out all the positive ones. For example, you had a great day at work. You completed your tasks ahead of schedule and were complimented for doing an efficient and thorough job. That evening, you focus only on the fact that you had all the work to do and forget about the compliment in its entirety.

- **Personalizing:** When something bad happens, you automatically make it personal. For example, if your friends cancel plans with you, you automatically assume that it's because they didn't want to hang out with you.

- **Assuming the worst:** You anticipate the worst without any indicator that the worst is going to transpire.

- **Blaming:** You try to say someone else is responsible for what happened to you instead of yourself.

Think about it—is your glass half-empty or half-full? How you answer this question about positive thinking may reflect your outlook on life, your attitude toward yourself, and whether you're actually optimistic or pessimistic. The truth is, though, that most of us can see it both as half-empty and half-full depending on our mood.

If you have had a particularly rough day and haven't had any food or drink, and you go to a diner for sustenance and are only met with a half-filled cup of drink and half a sandwich—are you likely to think of the cup as half-full or half-empty? Most people, in the heat of frustration, would see it as half-empty. Whereas others who have a more positive outlook on life may truly look at the cup and sandwich and be grateful for what they have. But those people would be in the vast minority. Especially since you're paying for a full sandwich and a full cup of your drink.

However, since the first step in positive thinking is to quiet the negative self-talk, we would squash any negative preconceived notions about the event that took place, and instead, we should all strive to look at everything positively, no matter what, and more times than not see the glass as half-full. This is controlled first by quieting that inner voice speaking negatively and also by regulating your emotions. Studies show that personality traits such as optimism and pessimism can affect many areas of your health and well-being. And being positive thinking doesn't mean that you ignore life's less pleasant situations (like getting that half-full drink when you paid for a full one). Positive thinking just means that you approach the situation in a more positive and productive way. Rather than become negative or frustrated, you could instead think the best will happen and ask the server for a little more drink. This sort of thinking usually starts with self-talk in the same way that negative self-talk starts—but it takes time, patience, and practice for those thoughts to be the first, or even the second, or even the third automatic thoughts we have.

Researchers continue to explore the effects of positive thinking and optimism on health. However, a conclusive list of benefits already shows that positive thinking may provide:

- Increased life span
- Lower rates of anxiety and depression
- Greater resistance to illnesses
- Genuinely better psychological and physical well-being
- Improved cardiovascular health and reduced risk of death from cardiovascular disease and stroke
- Reduced risk of death from cancer, respiratory conditions, or infections
- Better coping skills during hardships and times of stress

Although these benefits are clearly marked, it is not entirely clear yet why people who engage in this type of positive thinking experience these health benefits. There are theories, though, that having that outlook enables the person to cope better with stressful situations, which then reduces the harmful health effects that stress can have on your body.

It remains unclear why people who engage in positive thinking experience these health benefits. One theory is that having a positive outlook enables you to cope better with stressful situations, which reduces the harmful health effects of stress on your body.

So, start positive thinking by quieting your negative talk, and then follow one simple rule: don't say anything to yourself that you wouldn't say to anyone else. Be gentle and encouraging with yourself. If a negative thought enters your mind, evaluate it rationally and respond with affirmations. Things happen. Don't take it personally. The best thing you can do is respond appropriately and by looking at the bright side of things.

Always Work to Learn and Develop Yourself

You should always want to improve yourself. Every time you make a mistake, every time someone provides you with criticism, or any time you fail at something—it's important to take those as opportunistic lessons that can aid in your growth and development. Be positive about these experiences and truly see them as an area to develop yourself. It can sometimes feel overwhelming to figure out where—or even how—to start growing yourself beyond the point you are at in this very moment. But it's important to try. Take the feedback and criticisms and run with it. Prioritizing self-development can positively impact all areas of your life, but it can especially help you take on more responsibility in your professional life and launch your career forward. Some of the greatest ways to improve yourself professionally (and you can even tweak some of these for personal use, too) include:

- Read often
- Adopt as many new hobbies as you can
- Sign up for more training sessions or classes
- Identify in-demand skills and hone them
- Commit to an exercise routine
- Set big goals
- Find a mentor

Key Takeaways

Celebrating life is not just about cheering for ourselves but about cherishing every aspect of our existence, including loved ones and the experiences we have with them. Embracing each day with the mindset that it could be the best day of our lives—or even the last day of our lives— allows us to live with intention and gratitude. We are able to appreciate the surprises and uncertainties that come our way. By starting a gratitude journal, engaging in traditions, and spending quality time with our loved ones, we can cultivate deeper connections and find joy, even in the ordinary moments.

Learning to unwind and enjoy life, making every day special, and consciously working to maintain a positive mindset are essential practices for enhancing our overall well-being and finding fulfillment in our journey to love our life. Moreover, by making sure that we are also always prioritizing self-development through reading, learning new skills, setting goals, and seeking mentorship, we can ensure that we continually grow and evolve, unlocking new opportunities for personal *and* professional success. Ultimately, life is a precious gift meant to be celebrated, cherished, and lived to the fullest, one day at a time, and never forget that on your journey to love your life!

Chapter 8

Final Thoughts

In closing, let us reflect on the journey we've embarked on together—a journey of self-discovery, growth, and transformation. Throughout these pages, we've explored the profound wisdom of living life with intention, purpose, and, above all else, love. As we reach the final chapter, let these words serve as a gentle reminder to embrace each moment with gratitude and to cherish the relationships that enrich our lives, as well as prioritize them—and, moreover, ourselves—in mind, body, and spirit.

As we come to a close, it is important to remember that life is a precious gift, filled with countless opportunities for joy, connection, and fulfillment. Unfortunately, it is all too easy to get caught up in the busyness of daily life and lose sight of what truly matters. In these moments of disarray, it's essential to pause, breathe, and realign with our deepest values and desires. Our relationships—and ourselves.

So, as you navigate the twists and turns of life's journey, remember to:

- **Live in the moment:** Embrace each day with an open heart and a mindful presence. The past is but a memory, and the future is yet to unfold. The only moment we truly have is the present, so let us savor it fully and completely and live each and every day as though it was the best day ever—and even, potentially, our last.

- **Enjoy family and friends:** Cultivate meaningful connections with those who matter most in your life. Treasure the laughter, the tears, and the shared experiences that bind us together. For in the embrace of loved ones, we find strength, support, endless love and support, and a true sense of belonging.

- **Communicate needs and wants:** Honor your own truth, whatever it is, and express your needs with honesty and vulnerability. Communication is the foundation of healthy relationships, allowing us to build trust, intimacy, and understanding. Communicate your boundaries and limitations and trust the people you surround yourself with to respect them fully.

- **Work at being healthy:** Prioritize your well-being in body, mind, and spirit. Nurture your physical health with nourishing food, regular exercise, and adequate rest. Cultivate mental and emotional wellness through practices like mindfulness/prayer, self-care, and seeking support (whether through relationships or professional help) when needed.

- **And, above all else—love your life:** Embrace each day as a precious gift, a chance to love, to grow, and to become the fullest expression of yourself. Find joy in the simple moments, gratitude in the challenges, and beauty in the ordinary. For in loving our lives, we discover the true richness and abundance of the human experience.

As we bid farewell to this journey of discovering *50 Ways to Love Your Life*, may the words in this guide inspire you to live with passion, purpose, and profound gratitude. May you take your next walk a little slower, hug your loved ones a little longer, set aside purposeful time for yourself and for others, and truly enjoy life for the miracle that it is. May you embrace each day with an open heart and an unwavering commitment to love—both for yourself and those around you as you work on garnering a positive and uplifting outlook from this day onward.

About the Author

Dr. Sarah Cline lives with her husband, two daughters, two German Shepherds, and two Yorkies in the hills of North Carolina. Her expertise in relationship building has offered her the opportunity to travel around the world as a keynote speaker and international workshop facilitator.

www.ingramcontent.com/pod-product-compliance
Lightning Source LLC
Chambersburg PA
CBHW070110080526
44586CB00013B/1252